VOICES
from the
CIVIL WAR

Also by Milton Meltzer

Ain't Gonna Study War No More:
The Story of America's Peace Seekers

All Times, All Peoples:
A World History of Slavery

The American Revolutionaries:
A History in Their Own Words 1750–1800

The Black Americans:
A History in Their Own Words

A Book About Names

The Chinese Americans

The Hispanic Americans

The Jewish Americans:
A History in Their Own Words

Langston Hughes:
A Biography

Never to Forget:
The Jews of the Holocaust

Rescue: *The Story of How Gentiles
Saved Jews in the Holocaust*

The Terrorists

VOICES
from the
CIVIL WAR

A Documentary History of the
Great American Conflict

EDITED BY

Milton Meltzer

HarperTrophy
A Division of HarperCollins*Publishers*

Library of Congress Cataloging-in-Publication Data

Voices from the Civil War : a documentary history of the great
American conflict / edited by Milton Meltzer.
    p.   cm.
    Bibliography: p.
    Includes index.
    Summary: Letters, diaries, memoirs, interviews, ballads, newspaper
articles, and speeches depict life and events during the four years
of the Civil War.
    ISBN 0-690-04800-9. — ISBN 0-690-04802-5 (lib. bdg.)
    ISBN 0-06-446124-6 (pbk.)
    1. United States—History—Civil War,
1861–1865—Sources—Juvenile literature.
[1. United States—History—Civil War, 1861–1865.
2. United States—Social life and customs—Civil War, 1861–1865.]
I. Meltzer, Milton, date.
E464.V6   1989   88-34067
973.7—dc19   CIP
                                                AC

First Harper Trophy edition, 1992.

For Ruth and Harriet Clark

CONTENTS

FOREWORD

The Civil War of 1861–65 was the greatest crisis in America's life. It was a struggle for the future of our nation. Could the Southern states be permitted to secede from the Union? Would slavery be allowed to spread into the new territories of the West? Was the right to life, liberty, and the pursuit of happiness to be limited to whites only? These and other great questions were finally put to the test of arms, and settled in blood.

That war has roused more interest among readers than any other aspect of American history. The literature is enormous. It sees the war from many viewpoints: military, political, economic, social, constitutional, diplomatic, biographical.

This book—like my earlier *The American Revolutionaries: A History in Their Own Words, 1750–1800*—tries to help the reader understand the past from the point of view of the ordinary people, North and South, who lived through it. It tells, in their own words, what it was like to fight in the Union or Confederate forces. Since war is more than fighting, the book goes behind the lines to let us see what the folks back home saw in the light of their day. They did not stand aside and judge coolly, as historians do. Their words carry the passions and the prejudices of their time.

The whole canvas of the enormous conflict is not

covered here. It is far too broad to embrace in one fairly short book. And battle scenes, for one thing, are often too similar to bear repetition. So a considerable degree of selectivity was required to come up with the bits and pieces of human life—and death—that taken together may catch the spirit of the time. Letters, diaries, journals, memoirs, interviews, ballads, testimony in public hearings, speeches, make up this mosaic of that terrible conflict.

My method is to set the stage for each voice with a note about the person speaking and the events concerned. Many of the people of that time did not conform to any standard of spelling, punctuation, or paragraphing, so I have taken the liberty of modernizing their texts for easier reading. Cuts in the documents are indicated by ellipses (. . .). The source of each document is given at its end. The index will help the reader look up particular people, events, and topics.

VOICES from the CIVIL WAR

INTRODUCTION

THE CIVIL WAR was the climax of a struggle that had its roots deep in the American past. Ever since it began in 1861, people have argued over what caused the war. Some say it was not fought over slavery but over the question of states' rights. Some say it was really a conflict between the industrial power of the North and the agrarian power of the South for control of the government. Still others believe the North and the South had developed such different cultures and values that union between them was unnatural and could not last.

There is no simple explanation. As with any historical event, the underlying causes are many and complex. But in whatever explanation is offered, slavery is central. Without slavery the differences between North and South—in economy, in culture, in issues such as the tariff—would hardly have become so intensely focused as to ignite a war. It was slavery, says the historian David M. Potter, "that furnished the emotional voltage that led to deep distrust and dislike in each section for the people of the other."

In the colonies slavery was concentrated mainly in the South, where it became firmly fixed by the 1700s. North of Maryland slavery was not crucial to the economy, and it gradually disappeared. The slave system was wrapped in beliefs and practices rooted in racism. Excuses were

3

developed to justify the fat profits to be made from the slave trade and from the unpaid labor of black men and women and children. The slaveowners were "doing a kindness" by "civilizing" and "Christianizing" the ignorant and heathen Blacks. The myth of white supremacy gripped the minds of not only Southern whites but of Northern whites too. Every means of communication was used to spread the belief that the darker races were naturally inferior.

From the beginning, Blacks never accepted slavery. Their resistance took many forms, from running away to revolt. Some whites too believed slavery was wrong and formed groups to abolish bondage. When the American Revolution began, there were people who felt the deep contradiction between the professed belief in liberty and equal rights for all and the practice of enslaving Black Americans.

The decades before the Civil War saw a gradual shift of strength from a loosely organized agricultural society to a tightly organized modern industrial society. Along with this would come a change in government. Originally America was a group of states loosely tied together by a federal government, but the federal government was heading toward being a strongly centralized power in which the states would be less important subdivisions. The North's economy was racing past the South's, and the balance between them in political power was tipping toward the North.

It was a basic change, and the South did not like it. It greatly feared that a dominant North holding the levers of power would use that power to abolish slavery. Such a threat to the "Southern way of life"—to the foundation of

4

the South's economy and to white supremacy—was bound
to create a crisis.

That crisis was shaped and confronted in the decade of
the 1850s, which is where this story begins. . . .

∽ 1 ∽

TOO LATE FOR CAUTION

When the United States defeated Mexico in the war of 1846–47, the prize was one third of the Mexican Empire: California, New Mexico, Arizona, Nevada, Colorado, Utah. That was a turning point in history. The enormous territorial growth led the North and South to quarrel bitterly over the future of the new lands. Would the states to be carved out of them become slave or free? Only a few months after the Mexican War began, antislavery congressmen launched a campaign to keep new territories free. If they should succeed, Southerners knew that the spread of slavery would be checked and the political power of the slave states doomed. So Southerners denied Congress's right to interfere with slavery in the territories. They argued that the constitutional duty of Congress was to protect slave property in the territories. Only a territory itself, when it achieved statehood, could forbid slavery, the Southerners insisted.

In the 1848 election campaign both major parties, the Democrats and the Whigs, straddled the slavery issue. They gave the country a choice of Tweedledum or Tweedledee.

The result was the formation of a new party that had been taking shape for some time. Called the Free-Soil party, it was made up of antislavery men who left the other parties, and its banner flew the slogan of "Free Soil, Free Speech, Free Labor, and Free Men." While the Whigs elected General Zachary Taylor to the White House, the Free-Soil vote put thirteen men into the House of Representatives and gave them the balance of power between the Democrats and the Whigs.

As 1850 came in, a showdown seemed near between the antislavery and proslavery forces. Three issues stood out in the conflict: slavery in the territories; slavery and the slave trade in the District of Columbia; and the fugitive slaves who were finding shelter in Northern states.

Now California, applying for admission as a free state, took center stage. In the Union at this time were fifteen slave states and fifteen free states. California's admission would upset that balance. Some people, in and out of Con-

Abolitionists used the peace pledge to rally resistance to efforts to spread the power of slavery.

ANTI-SLAVERY PEACE PLEDGE.

WE, the undersigned,

hereby solemnly pledge ourselves not to countenance or aid the United States Government in any war which may be occasioned by the annexation of Texas, or in any other war, foreign or domestic, designed to strengthen or perpetuate slavery.

Name.	Residence.

gress, feared a showdown, and they called for caution. The antislavery congressman from Massachusetts Charles Hudson warned the Congress it was too late for caution:

YOU CANNOT JUDGE the present by the past. Within two years there has been a radical change in public sentiment in the free states. This iniquitous war [Mexican] . . . for the extension of slavery has brought the people to their senses. . . . The sentiment is deep-rooted; it is a strong religious conviction that slavery is a curse, and is at war with the best interests of our country and of humanity. A great moral revolution has commenced, and such revolutions can never go backward. . . . The people in the free states have resolved that the evil shall extend no farther. I say to the South in all frankness, you will find Northern sentiment immovable on the subject, "as firm as nature, and as fixed as fate."

From *Bound for the Rio Grande*, Milton Meltzer, Knopf, 1974.

The Southerners had become just as "immovable." Robert Toombs of Georgia rose in the Congress to say:

I DO NOT, then, hesitate to avow before this House and the country, and in the presence of the living God, that if by your legislation you seek to drive us from the territories of California and New Mexico, purchased by the common blood and treasure of the whole people, and to abolish slavery in this District, thereby attempting to fix a national degradation upon half the states of this Confederacy, I am for disunion; and if my physical courage be equal to the maintenance of my conviction of right and duty, I will devote all I am and all I have on earth to its consummation.

From *Bound for the Rio Grande*, Meltzer, 1974.

The threat of disunion, voiced often in the fevered debate, alarmed the great body of citizens. Could not some kind of give-and-take settle the issue and reduce the mounting sectional temperature? Senator Henry Clay answered the appeal. The Kentuckian was committed to preserving the Union and ready to conciliate the South to avoid a sectional clash. Early in 1850 he proposed a compromise. Congress would admit California as a free state while organizing Utah and New Mexico as territories without any restraint on slavery. Slave trading in the District of Columbia would be suppressed, but in return the South would be assured that there would be no interference with slavery itself in the District, or with the interstate slave trade, and that stronger measures for the return of fugitive slaves would be adopted.

Then Clay took the floor to speak out against the threat of secession:

IN MY OPINION there is no right on the part of any one or more of the states to secede from the Union. War and the dissolution of the Union are identical and inevitable, in my opinion. There can be a dissolution of the Union only by consent or by war. Consent no one can anticipate, from any existing state of things, is likely to be given; and war is the only alternative by which a dissolution could be accomplished. . . . And such a war as it would be, following the dissolution of the Union! Sir, we may search the pages of history, and none so ferocious, so bloody, so implacable, so exterminating . . . would rage with such violence . . . I implore gentlemen, I adjure them, whether from the South or the North . . . to pause at the edge of the precipice, before the fearful and dangerous leap be taken into the yawning abyss below, from which none who ever take it shall return in safety. . . .

From Clay's speech of Feb. 5–6, 1850, quoted in *Great Issues in American History*, Richard Hofstadter, Vintage, 1958.

In defiance of Clay, Senator John C. Calhoun of South Carolina, a dying man stubbornly insisting on the rights of slaveholders, wrote a speech that was read for him on the Senate floor. Rather disunion than compromise, he said. If California comes in free, the North will show it means to destroy forever the balance between the two sections. The only thing that can preserve the South's rights, he went on, is to amend the Constitution so as to convert the government into a federal alliance in which the majority could never impose its will upon the minority.

So extreme a proposal—to scrap the democratic principle of majority rule—pleased only a handful of the Southern fire-eaters.

After months of debate, and with the backing of such powerful politicians as the Whig Daniel Webster and the Democrat Stephen A. Douglas, Clay's compromise was voted into law in September 1850. Most citizens were relieved; they put their faith in peace. But some knew better. This "compromise," said Congressman Thaddeus Stevens, would become "the fruitful mother of future rebellion, disunion and civil war."

11

2

A FILTHY ENACTMENT—I WILL
NOT OBEY IT!

The passage of the Fugitive Slave Law, as part of the Compromise of 1850, caused the writer Ralph Waldo Emerson to cry out, "A filthy enactment; I will not obey it, by God!" Thousands of others in the North felt the law compelling the return of runaway slaves to their masters was a violation of the higher law of man's conscience and therefore not to be obeyed. When fugitives sought refuge in the North, many citizens gave moral or direct support to the men and women who dared harbor them.

In Pittsburgh, Frederick Douglass, himself a runaway slave and now the most prominent black leader, made a speech to a national Free-Soilers convention, denouncing the Whig and Democratic parties for their support of the law:

. . . BOTH NATIONAL CONVENTIONS acted in open contempt of the antislavery sentiment of the North, by incorporating, as the cornerstone of their two platforms, the infamous law to which I have alluded—a law which, I think, will never be repealed—it is too bad to be repealed—a law fit only to be trampled underfoot. The only way to make the Fugitive Slave Law a dead letter is to make half a dozen or more dead kidnappers. A half dozen more dead kidnappers carried down South would cool the

CAUTION!!
COLORED PEOPLE
OF BOSTON, ONE & ALL,

You are hereby respectfully CAUTIONED and advised, to avoid conversing with the

Watchmen and Police Officers of Boston,

For since the recent ORDER OF THE MAYOR & ALDERMEN, they are empowered to act as

KIDNAPPERS
AND
Slave Catchers,

And they have already been actually employed in KIDNAPPING, CATCHING, AND KEEPING SLAVES. Therefore, if you value your LIBERTY, and the *Welfare of the Fugitives* among you, *Shun* them in every possible manner, as so many *HOUNDS* on the track of the most unfortunate of your race.

Keep a Sharp Look Out for KIDNAPPERS, and have TOP EYE open.
APRIL 24, 1851.

A broadside prepared in April 1851 by the abolitionist preacher Theodore Parker, to warn blacks against Southerners hunting fugitive slaves in the streets of Boston. That same month Southerners captured Thomas Sims and took him back to slavery in Georgia.

ardor of Southern gentlemen, and keep their rapacity in check. That is perfectly right as long as the colored man has no protection. The colored men's rights are less than those of a jackass. No man can take away a jackass without submitting the matter to twelve men in any part of this country. A black man may be carried away without any reference to a jury. It is only necessary to claim him, and that some villain should swear to his identity. There is more protection there for a horse, for a donkey, or anything, rather than a colored man—who is, therefore, justified in the eye of God in maintaining his right with his arm. . . .

13

Human government is for the protection of rights; and when human government destroys human rights, it ceases to be a government, and becomes a foul and blasting conspiracy; and is entitled to no respect whatever. . . . If you look over the list of your rights, you do not find among them any right to make a slave of your brother.

Numbers should not be looked to so much as right. The man who is right is a majority. He who has God and conscience on his side, has a majority against the universe. Though he does not represent the present state, he represents the future state. If he does not represent what we are, he represents what we ought to be. . . .

From *Frederick Douglass's Paper*, August 1852.

Northern attacks on slavery made its Southern defenders ever more militant. One of the foremost apologists of slavery in the 1850s was the Virginian George Fitzhugh, editor and author. He claimed slavery was of benefit to both Southern whites and Blacks, and charged that Northern industrial workers were more insecure and worse exploited. Slavery would be good for the North too, he said, and he predicted that America must soon be either all slave or all free. These passages suggest the notions he circulated widely:

. . . THE EARLIEST CIVILIZATION of which history gives account is that of Egypt. The Negro was always in contact with that civilization. For four thousand years he has had opportunities of becoming civilized. Like the wild horse, he must be caught, tamed and domesticated. When his subjugation ceases he again runs wild, like the cattle on the Pampas of the South, or the horses on the prairies of the

14

THE BLACK LIST.

Total vote from free States in favor of the Fugitive Slave bill.

DEMOCRATS.—*Maine*--Messrs. Fuller, Gerry, Littlefield—3.

New Hampshire.—Messrs. HIBBARD and PEASLEE—2.

New York—Mr Walden—1.

New Jersey—Mr Wildrick—1.

Pennsylvania—Messr.s Dimmick, Job Mann, McLanahan, Robbins, Ross and James Thompson—6.

Ohio—Messrs. Hayland and Miller—2.

Indiana—Messrs, Alberston, William J. Brown, Dunham, Gorman, McDonald—5.

Illinois—Messrs. Bissel, T. L. Harris, McClernand, Richardson, Young—5.

Michigan—Mr A. W. Buel—1.

Iowa—Mr Leffier—1.

California—Mr Gilbert—1. Total 27.

WHIGS.—Messrs. Elliot, of *Mass.*; McGaughey, of *Ind.*; John L. Taylor, of *Ohio*—Total, 3.

Total Ayes from free states, 30.

This broadside of 1850 attacked free-state Congressmen who voted for the Fugitive Slave Act.

West. His condition in the West Indies proves this. . . .

But far the worst feature of modern civilization, which is the civilization of free society, remains to be exposed. Whilst laborsaving processes have probably lessened by one half, in the last century, the amount of work needed for comfortable support, the free laborer is compelled by capital and competition to work more than he ever did before, and is less comfortable. The organization of society cheats him of his earnings, and those earnings go to swell the vulgar pomp and pageantry of the ignorant millionaires, who are the only great of the present day. These reflections might seem, at first view, to have little connection with Negro slavery; but it is well for us of the South not to be deceived by the tinsel glare and glitter of free society, and to employ ourselves in doing our duty at home, and studying the past, rather than in insidious

15

rivalry of the expensive pleasures and pursuits of men whose sentiments and whose aims are low, sensual and groveling. . . .

The Southerner is the Negro's friend, his only friend. Let no intermeddling abolitionist, no refined philosophy, dissolve this friendship.

From *Sociology for the South*, George Fitzhugh, 1854.

∽ 3 ∾

A HOUSE DIVIDED CANNOT STAND

Four years after the Compromise of 1850, which many thought had settled the question of slavery's extension, Congress adopted the Kansas-Nebraska Act. It permitted voters in each territory to decide whether their new state would come into the Union with or without slavery. It launched a bloody battle in Kansas between proslavery and antislavery settlers. The violence warned how dangerously close to open warfare were the two opposing forces in the United States.

With "Bleeding Kansas" the chief campaign issue in the 1856 presidential election, the battle over slavery shifted to the ballot boxes. The Democrats elected James Buchanan, and the new Republican party's antislavery candidate, the explorer John C. Fremont, came in second, with Millard Fillmore, backed by the disintegrating Whigs and the Know-Nothings, in third place. The Republicans had gained great strength, alarming the South.

16

Then in March 1857 the Supreme Court handed down the Dred Scott decision. Scott, a slave, claimed that he was free because of temporary residence on free soil. Chief Justice Roger Taney's decision held that Scott was not a citizen, that no free Black had ever been one. Blacks, he went on, were "so far inferior that they had no rights which the white man was bound to respect." Going still deeper, Taney ruled that Congress had "no power to abolish or prevent slavery in any of the Territories." That decision denied all hope of justice for the Blacks. It made the slaveholders jubilant. But in the North and West great mass meetings were held in furious protest against the decision. White voters in ever greater numbers were driven toward the antislavery movement.

In 1858 Abraham Lincoln, an Illinois lawyer, upon winning the Republican nomination for the U.S. Senate, declared:

A HOUSE DIVIDED against itself cannot stand. I believe this government cannot endure permanently half-slave and half-free. I do not expect the Union to be dissolved—I do not expect the house to fall—but I do expect it will cease to be divided. It will become all one thing, or all the other. Either the opponents of slavery will arrest the further spread of it, and place it where the public mind shall rest in the belief that it is in the course of ultimate extinction, or its advocates will push it forward till it shall become alike lawful in all the States—old as well as new, North as well as South.

From *Words That Made American History*,
Richard N. Current and John A. Garraty, eds., 1965.

17

Violence builds in Kansas as Border Ruffians from Missouri invade the territory, determined to make it a slave state.

•

Senator Stephen Douglas, who wrote the Kansas-Nebraska law, is caricatured as a tough frontiersman ready to defend slavery in the territories.

In his series of seven celebrated debates with his Demo-cratic opponent, Stephen A. Douglas, author of the Kansas-Nebraska bill, Lincoln said:

YOU SAY SLAVERY is wrong; but don't you constantly argue that this is not the right place to oppose it? . . . It must not be opposed in politics, because that will make a fuss; it must not be opposed in the pulpit, because it is not religion. Then where is the place to oppose it?

In reply, Douglas said:

MR. LINCOLN TRIED to avoid the main issue by attacking the truth of my proposition, that our fathers made this government divided into free and slave states, recognizing the right of each to decide all its local questions for itself. Did they not thus make it? It is true they did not establish slavery in any of the States, or abolish it in any of them; but finding thirteen States, twelve of which were slave and one free, they agreed to form a government uniting them together, as they stood divided into free and slave States, and to guarantee forever to each State the right to do as it pleased on the slavery question. Having thus made the government, and conferred this right upon each State for-ever, I assert that this government can exist as they made it, divided into free and slave States, if any one State chooses to retain slavery. He says that he looks forward to a time when slavery shall be abolished everywhere. I look forward to a time when each State shall be allowed to do as it pleases. If it chooses to keep slavery forever, it is not my business, but its own; if it chooses to abolish slavery, it is its own business—not mine. I care more for the great principle of self-government, the right of the people to rule, than I do for all the Negroes in Christendom.

From *Words That Made American History*, Current and Garraty, 1965.

Though Douglas won the Senate seat, Lincoln gained a wide following and began a swift climb to national prominence.

～～4～～

HE TAUGHT US HOW TO LIVE

On the rainy Sunday night of October 16, 1859, John Brown with a band of twenty-one men attacked the federal arsenal at Harpers Ferry in Virginia (now West Virginia). His aim was to take the town, distribute arms to the slaves in the vicinity, and spread a slave revolt from there across the South. The arsenal was taken, but the plan failed. Two of Brown's sons were killed, as were eight other men, and Brown was wounded and taken prisoner with the rest.

When news of the raid was flashed to the country, it roused wild excitement. Southern cities called out troops for fear of slave uprisings. To the enemies of slavery it was "high noon." The poet Henry Wadsworth Longfellow called it "the day of a new revolution, quite as much needed as the old one." Ralph Waldo Emerson said Brown was "a new saint, who will make the gallows glorious like the cross." The black poet Frances E. W. Harper wrote, "Already from your prison has come a shout of triumph against the giant sin of our country."

Brown was tried for treason in a Virginia court, and sentenced to be hanged. In his last speech to the court he said these words:

I HAVE, may it please the Court, a few words to say. In the first place, I deny everything but what I have all along admitted, the design on my part to free the slaves. It is unjust that I should suffer such a penalty. Had I interfered in the manner which I admit, and which I admit has been fairly proved (for I admire the truthfulness and candor of the greater portion of the witnesses who have testified in this case), had I so interfered in behalf of the rich, the powerful, the intelligent, the so-called great, or in behalf of any of their friends—either father, mother, brother, sister, wife, or children, or any of that class, and suffered and sacrificed what I have in this interference, it would have been all right; and every man in this court would have deemed it an act worthy of reward rather than punishment.

This court acknowledges, as I suppose, the validity of the law of God. I see a book kissed here which I suppose to be the Bible, or at least the New Testament. That teaches me that all things whatsoever I would that men should do to me, I should do even so to them. It teaches me, further, to "remember them that are in bonds, as bound with them." I endeavored to act up to that instruction. I say, I am yet too young to understand that God is any respecter of persons. I believe that to have interfered

21

John Brown as he looked in 1859, when he led the raid on Harpers Ferry to strike a blow against slavery.

as I have done—as I have always freely admitted I have done—in behalf of His despised poor, was not wrong, but right. Now, if it is deemed necessary that I should forfeit my life for the furtherance of the ends of justice, and mingle my blood further with the blood of my children and with the blood of millions in this slave country whose rights are disregarded by wicked, cruel, and unjust enactments—I submit; so let it be done! . . .

From *A John Brown Reader*, Louis Ruchames, ed., 1959.

Brown was executed on December 2, 1859. Two years earlier, at lunch with Brown at his own family table in Concord, Massachusetts, Henry David Thoreau had discovered his "minority of one," a man of principle who would carry out the purpose of his life until the trap was sprung on his scaffold. Thoreau was deeply moved by Brown's bold deed, and in the Concord town hall he made the first public defense. No apology, it acclaimed the greatness of the man. Here are passages from "A Plea for Captain John Brown":

. . . I WISH I could say that Brown was the representative of the North. He was a superior man. He did not value his bodily life in comparison with ideal things. He did not recognize unjust human laws; but resisted them as he was bid. For once we are lifted out of the trivialness and dust of politics into the region of truth and manhood. No man in America has ever stood up so persistently and effectively for the dignity of human nature, knowing himself for a man, and the equal of any and all governments. In that sense he was the most American of us all. . . .

I hear many condemn these men because they were so few. When were the good and the brave ever in a majority?

Would you have had him wait till that time came?—till you and I came over to him? The very fact that he had no rabble or troop of hirelings about him would alone distinguish him from ordinary heroes. His company was small indeed, because few could be found worthy to pass muster. Each one who there laid down his life for the poor and oppressed was a picked man, culled out of many thousands, if not millions; apparently a man of principle, of rare courage, and devoted humanity; ready to sacrifice his life at any moment for the benefit of his fellow man. It may be doubted if there were as many more their equals in these respects in all the country—I speak of his followers only—for their leader, no doubt, scoured the land far and wide, seeking to swell his troops. These alone were ready to step between the oppressor and the oppressed. Surely they were the very best men you could select to be hung. That was the greatest compliment which this country could pay them. They were ripe for her gallows. She had tried a long time, she has hung a good many, but never found the right one before. . . .

These men, in teaching us how to die, have at the same time taught us how to live. If this man's acts and words do not create a revival, it will be the severest possible satire on the acts and words that do. It is the best news that America has ever heard. It has already quickened the feeble pulse of the North, and infused more and more generous blood into her veins and heart than any number of years of what is called commercial and political prosperity could. How many a man who was lately contemplating suicide has now something to live for!

From *Thoreau: People, Principles, and Politics*, Milton Meltzer, ed., 1963.

⟳ 5 ⟲

TWO PRESIDENTS

*As John Brown went to his grave, politicians in the Deep
South threatened that if a "Black Republican" won the
1860 presidential election, it would be grounds for secession. When the election campaign began, the Democratic
party split into two factions. The regular Democrats chose
Lincoln's old rival, Stephen A. Douglas, while the extreme
proslavery elements put up John Breckinridge of Kentucky.
The Republicans nominated Lincoln on a platform that,
though it did not call for the end of slavery, stood firmly
against any further extension of the slave system.*

*Southerners called the Republican party "a party of de-
struction." Cartoonists pictured Lincoln as about the ugli-
est man on earth. His friends replied that if every ugly man
voted for him, Lincoln would surely win. And he did win
in November. He took a majority of the electoral votes but
only some forty percent of the popular vote.*

*In that time presidents did not take office in January, as
they now do, but in March. And six weeks after Lincoln's
victory, South Carolina in convention cut all ties with the
Union. Shortly after, Mississippi, Florida, Alabama,
Georgia, and Louisiana all declared themselves no longer
a part of the United States. Under Calhoun's doctrine of
states' rights, they believed they had the right to withdraw
from the Union.*

In February 1861 the secessionists established a provi-

A campaign button for Jefferson Davis, elected president of the Confederate States of America.

sional government, called the Confederate States of America, and elected Jefferson Davis of Mississippi as its president.

What were the two presidents—Davis and Lincoln—like? William Russell of the London Times *was in America to report the news. He describes Davis in his diary:*

I HAD AN opportunity of observing the President very closely: He did not impress me as favorably as I had expected, though he is certainly a very different looking man from Mr. Lincoln. He is like a gentleman—has a slight light figure, little exceeding middle height, and holds himself erect and straight. He was dressed in a rustic suit of slate-colored stuff, with a black silk handkerchief round his neck; his manner is plain, and rather reserved and drastic; his head is well formed, with a fine full forehead, square and high, covered with innumerable fine lines and wrinkles, features regular, though the cheek-bones are too high, and the jaws too hollow to be hand-some; the lips are thin, flexible, and with wide nostrils; and the eyes deep-set, large and full—one seems nearly blind, and is partly covered with a film owing to excruciating attacks of neuralgia and tic. Wonderful to relate, he does not chew, and is neat and clean-looking, with hair trimmed, and boots brushed. The expression of his face is anxious, he has a very haggard, careworn, and pain-drawn look, though no trace of anything but the utmost confidence and the greatest decision could be detected in his conversation. He asked me some general questions respecting the route I had taken in the States.

From *My Diary North and South*, William Russell, 1863.

And now the impression Lincoln made on Nathaniel Hawthorne. The distinguished author of such books as The House of the Seven Gables, The Scarlet Letter, *and* Tanglewood Tales, *recently back home after seven years abroad, visited Lincoln in 1862 as part of a Massachusetts delegation:*

BY AND BY there was a little stir on the staircase and in the passageway, and in lounged a tall, loose-jointed figure, of an exaggerated Yankee port and demeanor, whom (as being about the homeliest man I ever saw, yet by no means repulsive or disagreeable) it was impossible not to recognize as Uncle Abe.

Unquestionably, Western man though he be, and Kentuckian by birth, President Lincoln is the essential representative of all Yankees, and the veritable specimen,

27

A Republican campaign poster of 1860. (Lincoln did not grow a beard until after the election.)

physically, of what the world seems determined to regard as our characteristic qualities. It is the strangest and yet the fittest thing in the jumble of human vicissitudes that he, out of so many millions, unlooked for, unselected by an intelligible process that could be based upon his genuine qualities, unknown to those who chose him, and unsuspected of what endowments may adapt him for his tremendous responsibility, should have found the way open for him to fling his lank personality into the chair of state, where, I presume, it was his first impulse to throw his legs on the council table and tell the Cabinet Ministers a story.

There is no describing his lengthy awkwardness nor the uncouthness of his movement; and yet it seemed as if I had been in the habit of seeing him daily, and had shaken hands with him a thousand times in some village street;

so true was he to the aspect of the pattern American, though with a certain extravagance which, possibly, I exaggerated still further by the delighted eagerness with which I took it in. If put to guess his calling and livelihood, I should have taken him for a country schoolmaster as soon as anything else. He was dressed in a rusty black frock coat and pantaloons, unbrushed, and worn so faithfully that the suit had adapted itself to the curves and angularities of his figure, and had grown to be an outer skin of the man. He had shabby slippers on his feet. His hair was black, still unmixed with gray, stiff, somewhat bushy, and had apparently been acquainted with neither brush nor comb that morning, after the disarrangement of the pillow; and as to a nightcap, Uncle Abe probably knows nothing of such effeminacies. His complexion is dark and sallow, betokening, I fear, an insalubrious atmosphere around the White House; he has thick black eyebrows and an impending brow, his nose is large, and the lines about his mouth are very strongly defined.

The whole physiognomy is as coarse a one as you would meet anywhere in the length and breadth of the States; but withal, it is redeemed, illuminated, softened, and brightened by a kindly though serious look out of his eyes, and an expression of homely sagacity, that seems weighted with rich results of village experience. A great deal of native sense; no bookish cultivation, no refinement; honest at heart, and thoroughly so, and yet, in some sort, sly—at least, endowed with a sort of tact and wisdom that are akin to craft, and would impel him, I think, to take an antagonist in flank, rather than to make a bull-run at him right in front. But, on the whole, I like this sallow, queer, sagacious visage, with the homely human sympathies that

29

warmed it; and, for my small share in the matter, would as lief have Uncle Abe for a ruler as any man whom it would have been practicable to put in his place.

Immediately on his entrance the President accosted our member of Congress, who had us in charge, and, with a comical twist of his face, made some jocular remark about the length of his breakfast. He then greeted us all round, not waiting for an introduction, but shaking and squeezing everybody's hand with the utmost cordiality, whether the individual's name was announced to him or not. His manner towards us was wholly without pretense, but yet had a kind of natural dignity, quite sufficient to keep the forwardest of us from clapping him on the shoulder and asking him for a story.

From *Tales, Sketches, and Other Papers,* Nathaniel Hawthorne.

A VISIT TO A SLAVE PLANTATION

Going to the South in 1861 to see firsthand what the people were like and how they lived, London Times *reporter William Russell observed the operation of the slave system. (Slavery had been abolished in England by a court decision of 1772, and the slave trade by an act of Parliament in 1807.) On a visit to a large sugar plantation in Louisiana, Russell entered these hardheaded notes in his diary on the economics of slavery:*

ADMITTING everything that can be said, I am the more persuaded from what I see, that the real foundation of slavery in the Southern states lies in the power of obtaining labor at will at a rate which cannot be controlled by any combination of the laborers. Granting the heat and the malaria, it is not for a moment to be argued that planters could not find white men to do their work if they would pay them for the risk. A Negro, it is true, bears heat well, and can toil under the blazing sun of Louisiana, in the stifling air between the thickset sugarcanes; but the Irishman who is employed in the stokehole of a steamer is exposed to a higher temperature and physical exertion even more arduous. The Irish laborer can, however, set a value on his work; the African slave can only determine the amount of work to be got from him by the exhaustion of his powers. Again, the indigo planter in India, out from morn till night amidst his ryots [peasants], or the sportsman toiling under the midday sun through swamp and jungle, proves that the white man can endure the utmost power of the hottest sun in the world as well as the native. . . .

It is in the supposed cheapness of slave labor and its profitable adaptation in the production of Southern crops, that the whole gist and essence of the question really lie. The planter can get from the labor of a slave for whom he has paid £200, a sum of money which will enable him to use up that slave in comparatively a few years of his life,

A Kentucky slave dealer's advertisement to buy slaves he can sell on the New Orleans market.

whilst he would have to pay to the white laborer a sum that would be a great apparent diminution of his profits, for the same amount of work. It is calculated that each field hand, as an able-bodied Negro is called, yields seven hogsheads of sugar a year, which, at the rate of fourpence a pound, at an average of a hogshead an acre, would produce to the planter £140 for every slave. This is wonderful interest on the planter's money; but he sometimes gets two hogsheads an acre, and even as many as three hogsheads have been produced in good years on the best lands; in other words, two and a quarter tons of sugar and

32

refuse stuff, called "bagasse," have been obtained from an acre of cane. Not one planter of the many I have asked has ever given an estimate of the annual cost of a slave's maintenance; the idea of calculating it never comes into their heads. . . .

The first place I visited with the overseer was a new sugarhouse, which Negro carpenters and masons were engaged in erecting. It would have been amusing, had not the subject been so grave, to hear the overseer's praises of the intelligence and skill of these workmen, and his boast that they did all the work of skilled laborers on the estate, and then to listen to him, in a few minutes, expatiating on the utter helplessness and ignorance of the black race, their incapacity to do any good, or even to take care of themselves. . . .

From *My Diary North and South*, Russell, 1863.

7

RUSH TO THE COLORS

Only five weeks after Lincoln took the oath of office, Confederate forces fired on Fort Sumter. The Civil War had begun. Lincoln declared that "insurrection" existed and called for seventy-five thousand three-month volunteers to put it down. Only a few saw at the time that this would be

no ninety-day war, but one that would bring many desper-
ate and costly battles. On both sides there was an emotional
rush to the colors, but very soon that patriotism cooled as
it became clear the war would drag on.

Many in the North were against using military power to
hold the Union together. In the South some still felt a
loyalty to the Union and believed this was a fight not for the
common good but only to protect the slaveholders' property.
The western counties of Virginia broke away from the state
and joined the Union as the new state of West Virginia. And
the border slave states of Missouri, Maryland, and Ken-
tucky remained loyal to the Union.

How did the people in the villages and cities react to the
news of the war? A young Georgian, Mrs. Mary A. Ward,
recalled it later, in testimony before a congressional com-
mittee:

THE DAY THAT Georgia was declared out of the Union
was a day of the wildest excitement in Rome. There was
no order or prearrangement about it at all, but the people
met each other and shook hands and exchanged congratu-
lations over it and manifested the utmost enthusiasm. Of
course a great many of the older and wiser heads looked
on with a great deal of foreboding at these rejoicings and
evidences of delight, but the general feeling was one of
excitement and joy.

Then we began preparing our soldiers for the war. The
ladies were all summoned to public places, to halls and
lecture rooms, and sometimes to churches, and everybody
who had sewing machines was invited to send them; they
were never demanded because the mere suggestion was
all-sufficient. The sewing machines were sent to these

Southern volunteers board a Confederate barge en route to the front. The South had 900,000 men of military age to draw on, the North 4,000,000.

places and ladies that were known to be experts in cutting out garments were engaged in that part of the work, and every lady in town was turned into a seamstress and worked as hard as anybody could work; and the ladies not only worked themselves but they brought colored seamstresses to these places, and these halls and public places would be filled with busy women all day long.

But even while we were doing all these things in this enthusiastic manner, of course there was a great deal of the pathetic manifested in connection with this enthusiasm, because we knew that the war meant the separation of our soldiers from their friends and families and the possibility of their not coming back. Still, while we spoke of these things, we really did not think that there was going to be actual war. We had an idea that when our soldiers got upon the ground and showed unmistakably that they were really ready and willing to fight—an idea that then, by some sort of hocus-pocus, we didn't know what, the whole trouble would be declared at an end. Of course we were not fully conscious of that feeling at the time, but that the feeling existed was beyond doubt from the great disappointment that showed itself afterwards when things turned out differently. We got our soldiers ready for the field, and the Governor of Georgia called out the troops and they were ordered out, five companies from Floyd County and three from Rome. They were ordered to Virginia under the command of General Joseph E. Johnston. The young men carried dress suits with them and any quantity of fine linen. . . .

Every soldier, nearly, had a servant with him, and a whole lot of spoons and forks, so as to live comfortably and elegantly in camp, and finally to make a splurge in Washington when they should arrive there, which they expected would be very soon indeed. That is really the way they went off; and their sweethearts gave them embroidered slippers and pincushions and needle-books, and all sorts of such little et ceteras, and they finally got off. . . .

From testimony of Mrs. Mary A. Ward,
in *Report of the Committee of the Senate upon
the Relations between Labor and Capital*, 1885, vol. IV, pp. 331–32.

Up in the North, in Indiana, Theodore Upson, sixteen, heard the news while working in the fields with his father:

FATHER AND I were husking out some corn. We could not finish before it wintered up. When William Cory came across the field (he had been down after the mail) he was excited and said, "Jonathan, the Rebs have fired upon and taken Fort Sumter." Father got white and couldn't say a word.

William said, "The President will soon fix them. He has called for 75,000 men and is going to blockade their ports, and just as soon as those fellows find out that the North means business, they will get down off their high horse."

Father said little. We did not finish the corn and drove to the barn. Father left me to unload and put out the team and went to the house. After I had finished I went in to dinner. Mother said, "What is the matter with Father?" He had gone right upstairs. I told her what we had heard. She went to him. After a while they came down. Father looked ten years older. We sat down to the table. Grandma wanted to know what was the trouble. Father told her and she began to cry: "Oh, my poor children in the South! Now they will suffer! God knows how they will suffer! I knew it would come! Jonathan, I told you it would come!"

"They can come here and stay," said Father.

"No, they will not do that. There is their home. There they will stay. Oh, to think that I should have lived to see the day when Brother should rise against Brother."

She and Mother were crying and I lit out for the barn. I do hate to see women cry.

We had another meeting at the schoolhouse last night; we are raising money to take care of the families of those who enlist. A good many gave money, others subscribed. The Hulper boys have enlisted and Steve Lampman and

37

some others. I said I would go but they laughed at me and said they wanted men not boys for this job; that it would all be over soon; that those fellows down South are big bluffers and would rather talk than fight. I am not so sure about that. I know the Hale boys would fight with their fists at any rate and I believe they would fight with guns too if needs be. I remember how Charlie would get on our Dick and ride on a gallop across our south field cutting mullin heads with his wooden sword playing they were Indians or Mexicans (his father was in the Mexican War), and he looked fine. To be sure there was no danger, but I feel pretty certain he could fight. Maybe it won't be such a picnic as some say it will. There has been a fight down in Virginia at Big Bethel. Al Beecher's nephew was in it and wrote to his uncle and he read the letter in his store. I could not make out which side whipped but from the papers I think the Rebels had the best of it. Mother had

A Northern recruiting poster offering pay and prize money for sailors who sign up.

a letter from the Hales. Charlie and his father are in their army and Dayton wanted to go but was too young. I wonder if I were in our army and they should meet me would they shoot me. I suppose they would.

From *With Sherman to the Sea:*
The Civil War Letters, Diaries & Reminiscences of Theodore F. Upson,
Oscar O. Winthur, ed., Louisiana State University Press, 1943.

The war fever seized Warren Lee Goss of Massachusetts when he heard the news that one of his state's regiments, headed for Washington, had been mobbed by Confederate sympathizers as the soldiers passed through Baltimore:

"COLD CHILLS" ran up and down my back as I got out of bed after the sleepless night, and shaved preparatory to other desperate deeds of valor. I was twenty years of age, and when anything unusual was to be done, like fighting or courting, I shaved.

With a nervous tremor convulsing my system, and my heart thumping like muffled drumbeats, I stood before the door of the recruiting office, and before turning the knob to enter read and reread the advertisement for recruits posted thereon, until I knew all its peculiarities. The promised chances for "travel and promotion" seemed good, and I thought I might have made a mistake in considering war so serious after all. "Chances for travel!" I must confess now, after four years of soldiering, that the "chances for travel" were no myth; but "promotion" was a little uncertain and slow.

I was in no hurry to open the door. Though determined to enlist, I was half inclined to put if off awhile; I had a fluctuation of desires; I was fainthearted and brave; I wanted to enlist, and yet— Here I turned the knob, and was relieved. . . .

My first uniform was a bad fit: My trousers were too long by three or four inches; the flannel shirt was coarse and unpleasant, too large at the neck and too short elsewhere. The forage cap was an ungainly bag with pasteboard top and leather visor; the blouse was the only part which seemed decent; while the overcoat made me feel like a little nubbin of corn in a large preponderance of husk. Nothing except "Virginia mud" ever took down my ideas of military pomp quite so low.

After enlisting I did not seem of so much consequence as I had expected. There was not so much excitement on account of my military appearance as I deemed justly my due. I was taught my facings, and at the time I thought the drillmaster needlessly fussy about shouldering, ordering, and presenting arms. At this time men were often drilled in company and regimental evolutions long before they learned the manual of arms, because of the difficulty of obtaining muskets. These we obtained at an early day, but we would willingly have resigned them after carrying them a few hours. The musket, after an hour's drill, seemed heavier and less ornamental than it had looked to be.

The first day I went out to drill, getting tired of doing the same things over and over, I said to the drill sergeant: "Let's stop this fooling and go over to the grocery." His only reply was addressed to a corporal: "Corporal, take this man out and drill him like hell"; and the corporal did! I found that suggestions were not so well appreciated in the army as in private life, and that no wisdom was equal to a drillmaster's "Right face," "Left wheel," and "Right, oblique, march." It takes a raw recruit some time to learn that he is not to think or suggest, but obey. Some never do learn. I acquired it at last, in humility and mud, but it was tough. Yet I doubt if my patriotism, during my first three weeks' drill, was quite knee high. Drilling looks easy to a spectator, but it isn't. After a time I had cut down my uniform so that I could see out of it, and had conquered the drill sufficiently to see through it. Then the word came: On to Washington! . . .

From *Recollections of a Private: A Story of the Army of the Potomac*,
Warren Lee Goss, Crowell, 1890.

THE GLITTER OF BAYONETS

Why did men volunteer? In the North, many did it because they saw their friends do it. Some did it because though soldier pay was low, so were wages. And the army meant steady work, especially for the recently arrived two million immigrants, many of whom joined up. When conscription began, it looked better to volunteer than to be drafted. Of course faith in the Union and a sense of duty to it, and hatred for the "traitors" who wanted to destroy it, brought many to enlist. Some fought to free the slaves, but historians estimate that maybe only one out of ten men took up arms for that reason. During the course of the war a number of soldiers who had never thought about slavery came to support emancipation. "Slavery must die," wrote one Vermont corporal, "and if the South insists on being buried in the same grave I shall see nothing in it but the retributive hand of God." Then too, remember that a great many people expected the Rebels to be licked quickly, and they wanted to be part of the one and only fight.

Southerners showed the same eagerness to go off to war, and also from a mix of motives. Some hated the Yankees because of their refusal to cooperate with the return of fugitive slaves and their passionate attacks upon the "peculiar institution" of slavery. They charged that the enormously popular novel about slavery, Uncle Tom's Cabin, *was fantasy, not reality. People who had hoped for compromise and peace had no choice left when Fort Sumter was attacked. The heated agitation for secession whipped up a readiness to fight for states' rights.*

But the evidence shows that many Southern volunteers, like soldiers everywhere, were simply out for adventure, for a change from the lonely seasons behind a plow or the dull days behind a store counter. And like many Northerners, many Confederates enlisted because it was the thing to do.

On July 21 came the first big battle. The Union forces were routed at Bull Run. The North had been confident of success in this move toward the Confederate capital at Richmond. News of the defeat was a stunning surprise. Abner Small was with a company of Maine Volunteers as it headed for its first engagement at Bull Run. He tells what happened to him:

42

OUR BRIGADE was left behind in reserve. We stayed in that woods road four mortal hours, longer hours than I had ever known. The battle was begun within our hearing but beyond our sight. It was stifling hot; not a breath of air was stirring. Our flags hung limp. I think it was while we were waiting in this place that we knelt and repeated the Lord's Prayer. The long suspense fretted us. Our nerves jumped.

Shortly after noon a mounted officer came dashing out of the woods and drew rein where Colonel Howard was fidgeting. There was a sudden stir, a shouting of orders, and we started up the forest track. We marched through the woods and came to an open flat, where Lieutenant Burt met us and told our commander that we were to hurry. We went on at the double quick, but a mile of this was all that we could do; the heat and the fretting of our long wait had weakened us; men dropped, exhausted and fainting, by the wayside. Another mile, and another, we hurried on at quick time; this meant double quick at the rear, and we lost other stragglers. Men still on their feet and pressing forward threw away their blankets, their haversacks, their coats, even their canteens. When we got to Bull Run at Sudley's Ford, many stopped to drink; scooped up muddy water in their hands, their hats, their shoes, drank too much; were lost to service for that day. Not half the brigade, nor half the regiment, crossed the run.

Beyond the stream, we went up through a scattering of trees and came out into cleared lands. We passed an improvised hospital near Sudley Church. I can see today, as I saw then, the dead and hurt men lying limp on the ground. Up the road from ahead of us came ambulances filled with wounded. Farther away there were rattles of musketry and the quick and heavy thuddings of artillery. Puffs of white smoke and straggling clouds of dust rose wavering into the still air. There was the battle, and we were coming to it late; it must have been near three o'clock, by then.

We hurried on, down the road and off obliquely to our right through the fields. When at last we neared the scene of battle, broken regiments and scattering stragglers were drifting back. We pushed on across the Warrenton turnpike, splashed through the muddy shallows of Young's Branch, and turned to our left in a ravine; and there, under cover of the trees and bushes that screened its farther slope, we caught our breath and wondered for the last time, confusedly, what it was going to be like to face fire. The brigade was now formed in two lines, the 4th Maine and 2nd Vermont regiments ahead, the 5th and 3rd Maine behind. Up through the trees Colonel Howard led the forward line, out of our sight; and we that were left waiting had a last anxious quarter hour. We felt that our numbers were very few and we wanted company.

Where were the brigades that we had come to support? We didn't know that they had been flung, regiment by regiment, up the slope, vain efforts to support or bring off the guns of two batteries. Those guns had been lost and recovered and lost again, and back and forth over the field where they stood unlimbered, the gunners lying dead around them, the battle had been hardest fought. Colonel Howard, going up with his first line, met an officer "with his face all covered with blood, on a horse that had been shot through the nose." This was the only officer surviving, not disabled, of one of the lost batteries. He was

The rout of the Union troops at Bull Run.

bringing off a caisson, and this was to give rise to a rumor, afterwards, that our brigade was sent up in support of a battery that was leaving the field.

Some cavalrymen, pelting for the rear, broke the ranks of the 5th Maine, and carried away some of the wreckage in their blundering flight. From off to the right a rebel battery opened fire, and the survivors of the unhappy 5th suffered more damage and disorder, a ball striking their flank.

Colonel Howard came back for his second line, and up we scrambled. The next thing we knew, we were in the field on the hill and facing the enemy. I can only recall that we stood there and blazed away. There was a wild uproar of shouting and firing. The faces near me were inhuman. From somewhere across the field a battery pounded us; in the hot, still air the smoke of the cannon clung to the ground before it lifted; and through the smoke, straight ahead of us, flashed and crackled the rebel musketry. We didn't see our foes; they were obscured in smoke and trees. We felt that our lines were needlessly exposed, and weak without cannon to return blow for blow. David Bates, one of my close comrades, was smashed by a solid shot; and what reply could we make to that? We wavered, and rallied, and fired blindly; and men fell writhing, and others melted from sight; and we saw the glitter of bayonets coming against our flank; and we heard the order to retire. It was the turn of the tide.

From *The Road to Richmond:*
The Civil War Memoirs of Major Abner R. Small,
Harold Adams Small, ed., University of California Press, 1957.

9

SCREAMING, FIGHTING, DYING

The Civil War would last four years, from April 1861 to April 1865. When it began, the balance of opposing forces was very uneven. The North: twenty-three states with twenty-two million people, strong industry and agriculture and finance, a railroad system linking all its parts, and a good merchant marine. The South: eleven states with nine million people (a third of them slaves), a plantation economy, limited industry, scanty financial resources, a thin railroad grid, rivers and valleys that made invasion from the North easier, and only a few good harbors, easily block-aded.

Then how could the South think it could win? Because it had contempt for the North and blind pride in itself. The North wouldn't put up a real fight, many Rebels believed. The South only had to stand strong on the defensive, and the North would get sick of losing battles and call it quits. Besides, Great Britain and France, depending on Southern staples, would recognize the Confederacy and give it help.

Drawing on its far bigger pool of manpower, the North mustered two million men, the South only eight hundred thousand. Still, the North faced a much harder military task. It had to conquer and control a region bigger than all of western Europe. Problems of supply and communication were immensely difficult. Here the North's superior rail-road network was of crucial value.

Few people on either side had much experience of war, or even grasped, at this early stage, the vast difficulties of recruiting, equipping, training, and maintaining great armies. It was amateur versus amateur in the beginning.

The fighting would sweep over half the country, touching every slave state but Delaware and reaching up into five of the Northern states. The main battleground, however, was the Virginia front. The Confederate capital, moved to Rich-mond, was only one hundred miles south of Washington. So the Union aimed to capture it while the South struggled to defend it. On that Virginia front the Union endured a trail of defeats for two long years, beginning with the Union disaster at Bull Run. That battle made Thomas "Stone-wall" Jackson a Confederate hero. In a letter to his wife written two days later, he gives credit to God for the victory:

MY PRECIOUS PET,

Yesterday we fought a great battle and gained a great victory, for which all the glory is due to God alone. Although under a heavy fire for several continuous hours, I received only one wound, the breaking of the longest finger of my left hand; but the doctor says the finger can be saved. It was broken about midway between the hand and knuckle, the ball passing on the side next the forefinger. Had it struck the center, I should have lost the finger. My horse was wounded, but not killed. Your coat got an ugly wound near the hip, but my servant, who is very handy, has so far repaired it that it doesn't show very much. My preservation was entirely due, as was the glorious victory, to our God, to whom be all the honor, praise and glory. The battle was the hardest that I have ever been in, but not near so hot in its fire. I commanded the center more particularly, though one of my regiments extended to the right for some distance. There were other commanders on my right and left. Whilst great credit is due to other parts of our gallant army, God made my brigade more instrumental than any other in repulsing the main attack. This is for your information only—say nothing about it. Let others speak praise, not myself.

From *Life and Letters of General Thomas J. Jackson*, M. Jackson, ed., Harper, 1891.

Jackson was a general, Randolph A. Shotwell a seventeen-year-old private in the Confederate ranks. Fighting with the 8th Virginia, he helped beat the Union army at Ball's Bluff on October 21, 1861. He describes the effect of a terrific volley against the enemy that ended the battle:

Confederate and Union troops fighting at close quarters in the Shenandoah Valley.

THEN ENSUED an awful spectacle! A kind of shiver ran through the huddled mass upon the brow of the cliff; it gave way; rushed a few steps; then, in one wild, panic-stricken herd, rolled, leaped, tumbled over the precipice! The descent is nearly perpendicular, with ragged, jutting crags, and a water-laved base. Screams of pain and terror filled the air. Men seemed suddenly bereft of reason; they leaped over the bluff with muskets still in their clutch, threw themselves into the river without divesting themselves of their heavy accoutrements, hence went to the bottom like lead. Others sprang down upon the heads and bayonets of those below. A gray-haired private of the First California was found with his head mashed between two rocks by the heavy boots of a ponderous "Tammany" man, who had broken his own neck by the fall! The side of the bluff was worn smooth by the number sliding down.

From the beginning of the battle a steady stream of wounded men had been trickling down the zigzag path leading to the narrow beach, whence the boats were to convey them to the island. As it happened, the two larger bateaux were just starting with an overload when the torrent of terror-stricken fugitives rolled down the bluffs— upon them. Both boats were instantly submerged, and their cargoes of helpless human beings (crippled by wounds) were swept away to unknown graves! The whole surface of the river seemed filled with heads, struggling, screaming, fighting, dying! Man clutched at man, and the strong, who might have escaped, were dragged down by the weaker. Voices that strove to shout for help were stifled by the turbid, sullen waters of the swollen river and died away in gurgles. It is strange how persons about to drown turn to their fellows for strength; they may be in mid-ocean, with no hope for any, yet will they grasp one another and sink in pairs. Captain Otter, of the First California (an apposite name for a swimmer), was found a few days later with two men of his company clutching his neckband. Had he attempted to save them, or had they seized him and dragged him down? One officer was found with $126 in gold in his pocket; it had cost his life.

From *The Papers of Randolph Abbott Shotwell*, J. G. Roulhac Hamilton, ed., North Carolina Historical Commission, 1929.

10

THEY RAN TO FREEDOM

Its defeat at Bull Run scared the North. If the Rebels could do so well, the capital at Washington was itself in danger. Lincoln realized that an invasion of the South called for a far larger and more permanent and better trained army than the three-month volunteers who could go home whenever their term of enlistment was up—even on the eve of battle! He named George B. McClellan commanding general to do the job. For almost a year there was no fighting on the Virginia front. Then in April 1862 McClellan carried his troops by sea to Fort Monroe on the Virginia coast, within striking distance of Richmond. His aim was to move up the peninsula between the York and James rivers and to capture the Confederate capital.

In the first year of the war thousands of slaves fled their masters and headed for the Union lines. There lay safety and freedom. They believed Lincoln was their friend and that his soldiers would protect them. Since there was no government ruling on what to do with such Blacks, each commander did as he wished. Some protected the runaways, others ignored them or even returned them to their masters. (This while knowing the Confederates used them for military labor.) But Washington gradually moved to bar the return of such "contrabands." They served the Union as laborers, scouts, spies, guides, cooks, blacksmiths, mule drivers, hospital workers.

51

So while this was not yet officially a war to free the slaves, Union troops inevitably became liberators. Wherever they advanced into slave territory, black men, women, children, the old, the aged, and the infirm met freedom. But for many this did not mean comfort or security. Harriet Jacobs, a North Carolina slave who escaped long before the war, went down to Washington in the spring of 1862 to see what help the contrabands needed. She found hundreds of homeless and hungry people, a number that would swell to forty thousand by the war's end. In a letter to The Liberator *Jacobs describes their needs, and appeals for help:*

I WENT TO Duff Green's Row, government headquarters for the contrabands here. I found men, women and children all huddled together without any distinction or regard to age or sex. Some of them were in the most pitiable condition. Many were sick with measles, diphtheria, scarlet and typhoid fever. Some had a few filthy rags to lie on, others had nothing but the bare floor for a couch. They were coming in at all times, often through the night, and the Superintendent had enough to occupy his time in taking the names of those who came in and those who were sent out. His office was thronged through the day by persons who came to hire the poor creatures. Single women hire at four dollars a month, a woman with one child two and a half or three dollars a month. Men's wages are ten dollars per month. Many of them, accustomed as they have been to field labor, and to living almost entirely out of doors, suffer much from the confinement in this crowded building. The little children pine like prison birds for their native element. It is almost impossible to keep the building in a healthy condition. Each day brings the fresh additions of the hungry, naked and sick.

Hoping to help a little in the good work, I wrote to a lady in New York, a true and tried friend of the slave, to ask for such articles as would make comfortable the sick and dying in the hospital. On the Saturday following an immense box was received from New York. Before the sun went down, I had the satisfaction of seeing every man, woman and child with clean garments, lying in a clean bed. What a contrast! They seemed different beings.

Alexandria is strongly Secesh [Secessionist]; the inhabitants are kept quiet only at the point of Northern bayonets. In this place, the contrabands are distributed more over the city. The old schoolhouse is the Government headquarters for the women. This I thought the most wretched of all. In this house are scores of women and children with nothing to do, and nothing to do with. Their husbands are at work for the Government. Here they have food and shelter, but they cannot get work. . . .

My first visit for Alexandria was on a Saturday. To the very old people I gave some clothing. Begging me to come back, they promised to do all they could to help themselves.

From The Liberator, September 3, 1862.

Many Northerners responded to such appeals for help. This letter from Lydia Maria Child, the abolitionist author, indicates some of the things they did. It is written to Helen F. Garrison:

DEAR FANNY,

My big box was sent off to the "contrabands" on Monday morning, and your letter arrived Monday evening. I did see the statement in the papers that Government intended to give each of the fugitives a "plantation suit." But there seemed to be no official authority for the statement; moreover, a "plantation suit" does not sound very comfortable, in view of approaching winter. It is also stated in the papers that the Government have recently resolved to pay the "contrabands" in their employ; but I find that their friend, Edward L. Pierce, doubts whether there is official ground for this; and even if there is, the Government will pay wages only to those they employ, and many of them are not employed by the U.S. but scramble for a living as they best can.

Rev. L. C. Lockwood, the missionary among them . . . describes them as generally a sober, industrious, religious people, and many of them very intelligent. I have had three letters from him. He says they do need assistance, and will suffer for clothing and bedding this winter unless the charitable extend a helping hand. . . . People are so busy giving and working for the soldiers that few think of the poor fugitives. In answer to my questions, he informed me that some of the women could cut and make garments, and that many of them were good knitters. So I sent thread, tape, buttons, needles, and knitting needles etc. with the new cloth. I bought $15 worth of flannel and calico, and for a fortnight worked as hard as I could drive, repairing secondhand garments . . . and making hoods for the women, and woollen caps for the men, out of such pieces as I could muster.

Mrs. Stevenson gave me various secondhand articles of clothing for children, one pair of woollen socks, and 20 picture books, and primary schoolbooks. Mrs. Sears made a similar contribution. I restitched many of the books, and

Thousands of slaves fled the plantations at the first opportunity to escape and headed for Union army camps.

enclosed them in good strong covers. I gathered up all the biographies of runaway slaves that I could find. I bound them anew. . . . These and a copy of *Uncle Tom's Cabin* I did up in separate parcels. My good Henrietta gave me $10 in money to be expended for whatever the "contrabands" most needed. She also sent 5 books, 7 pair of woollen socks, and two woollen shirts. A friend in Weston sent me 30 yds of white cotton flannel and 21 skeins of yarn. I left it to the missionary to distribute the clothing and schoolbooks according to his judgment. . . . If the poor creatures have half as much satisfaction in receiving the contents as I had in buying, making and repairing, I shall be glad. . . .

From *Lydia Maria Child: Selected Letters, 1817–1880*, Milton Meltzer and Patrica Holland, eds., University of Massachusetts Press, 1982.

A New Jersey Quaker, Cornelia Hancock, twenty-three, went south to a Washington hospital for contrabands to work as a nurse. In this letter to her sister she tells what she saw and did:

MY DEAR SISTER:

I shall depict our wants in true but ardent words, hoping to affect you to some action. Here are gathered the sick from the contraband camps in the northern part of Washington. If I were to describe this hospital, it would not be believed. North of Washington, in an open, muddy mire, are gathered all the colored people who have been made free by the progress of our Army. Sickness is inevitable, and to meet it these rude hospitals, only rough wooden barracks, are in use—a place where there is so much to be done you need not remain idle. We average here one birth per day, and have no baby clothes except as we wrap them up in an old piece of muslin, that even being scarce. Now the Army is advancing, it is not uncommon to see from 40 to 50 arrivals in one day. They go at first to the camp but many of them being sick from exhaustion soon come to us. They have nothing that anyone in the North would call clothing. I always see them as soon as they arrive, as they come here to be vaccinated; about 25 a day are vaccinated.

This hospital is the reservoir for all cripples, diseased, aged, wounded, infirm, from whatsoever cause; all accidents happening to colored people in all employs around Washington are brought here. A woman was brought here with three children by her side; said she had been on the road for some time; a more forlorn, wornout-looking creature I never beheld. Her four eldest children are still in

56

slavery, her husband is dead. When I first saw her she laid on the floor, leaning against a bed, her children crying around her. One child died almost immediately, the other two are still sick. She seemed to need most food and rest, and those two comforts we gave her, but clothes she still wants. . . .

I ask for clothing for women and children, both boys and girls. Two little boys; one 3 years old, had his leg amputated above the knee, the cause being his mother not being allowed to ride inside, became dizzy and had dropped him. The other had his leg broken from the same cause. This hospital consists of all the lame, halt, and blind escaped from slavery. We have a man and woman here without any feet, theirs being frozen so they had to be amputated. Almost all have scars of some description and many have very weak eyes.

From *South After Gettysburg:
Letters of Cornelia Hancock from the Army of the Potomac, 1863–1865*,
Henrietta Jacquette, ed., University of Pennsylvania Press, 1937.

11

SONGS OF THE SOLDIERS

*Out of the Civil War came many topical songs, often written
not by professionals but by anonymous Americans, and
usually set to old ballad tunes. Many were printed on
broadsides, to find their way into camp and field and home.
The more popular and enduring ones were published in
sheet music and songbooks.*

*The songs respond to the events of the moment—a sol-
dier's leaving home, life in the training camps, the agony
of the battlefield, the celebration of victories. The most
popular marching song of the Union armies was "John
Brown's body lies a-mould'ring in the grave," written by
Thomas Bishop. Early in the war, while visiting Washington, the abolitionist Julia Ward Howe heard the song and
wrote new words to the tune. Known as the "Battle Hymn
of the Republic," it swept the North and has remained one
of the most stirring American songs:*

> Mine eyes have seen the glory of
> the coming of the Lord;
> He is trampling out the vintage
> where the grapes of wrath are stored;
> He hath loosed the fateful lightning
> of His terrible swift sword,
> His truth is marching on.

I have seen Him in the watch-fires
of a hundred circling camps;
They have builded Him an altar
in the evening dews and damps;
I can read His righteous sentence
by the dim and flaring lamps,
His day is marching on.

I have read a fiery gospel, writ in
burnished rows of steel:
"As ye deal with my contemners, so
with you my grace shall deal;
Let the Hero, born of woman, crush the serpent
with his heel,
Since God is marching on."

He has sounded forth the trumpet
that shall never call retreat;
He is sifting out the hearts of men
before His judgment-seat;
Oh, be swift, my soul, to answer Him!
be jubilant, my feet!
Our God is marching on.

In the beauty of the lilies Christ was born
across the sea,
With a glory in His bosom that
transfigures you and me:
As He died to make men holy, let us die
to make men free,
While God is marching on.

As any war does, this one produced sentimental songs that the troops loved to sing about home, mother, and sweethearts.

Maryland, one of the border slave states, wavered when the war began. As Federal troops marched through Baltimore in the first days of the war, they were attacked by Southern sympathizers. But the state did not secede. The Baltimorean James R. Randall, who urged secession, wrote the famous song "My Maryland," sung to the tune of "O Tannenbaum." It became the most popular marching song of the Confederate soldiers. These are the opening and closing stanzas:

> The despot's heel is on thy shore,
> Maryland!
> His torch is at thy temple door,

Maryland!
Avenge the patriotic gore
That flecked the streets of Baltimore,
And be the battle-queen of yore,
  Maryland, My Maryland!

Hark to an exiled son's appeal,
  Maryland!
My Mother State, to thee I kneel,
  Maryland!
For life and death, for woe and weal,
Thy peerless chivalry reveal,
And Gird thy beauteous limbs with steel,
  Maryland, My Maryland!

. . .

Thou wilt not yield the Vandal toll,
  Maryland!
Thou wilt not crook to his control,
  Maryland!
Better the fire upon thee roll,
Better the shot, the blade, the bowl,
Than crucifixion of the soul,
  Maryland, My Maryland!

I hear the distant thunder hum,
  Maryland!
The Old Line's bugle, fife, and drum,
  Maryland!
She is not dead, nor deaf, nor dumb;
Huzza! she spurns the Northern scum!
She breathes! She burns! She'll come! She'll come!
  Maryland, My Maryland!

12

SLOW TORTURE

Winter was no time for fighting on either side. Most of the campaigns ranged over the northern part of the Confederacy, and winters there were not only cold but wet and sometimes snowy. Army leaders shunned action under such conditions. When cold weather came, they looked for good quarters for their troops. The men needed wood and water and drainage and access to supplies. They put up log huts or tents and, as a last resort, holed up in dugouts.

As weeks dragged into months soldiers became sick of the confinement and idleness. Tempers flared, quarrels erupted, fistfights broke out, discipline slacked off. To break the monotony, many read books and newspapers and gave hours to writing letters home. They went to prayer meetings and revivals, played cards, skated, sledded, let off steam in fierce snowball battles that whole brigades joined in. If there was a town or village nearby, visiting with the local folk helped break the boredom.

With the arrival of better weather the fighting resumed. McClellan's campaign on the Virginia peninsula got started in the summer of 1862. His forces outnumbered General Robert E. Lee's Confederates, but his tactics failed, and the Federals had to retreat. Oliver Norton, a private of the 83rd Regiment, Pennsylvania Volunteers, wrote home about the battle of Gaines' Mill:

THE ORDER was given to face about. We did so and tried to form in line, but while the line was forming, a bullet laid low the head, the stay, the trust of our regiment—our brave colonel, and before we knew what had happened the major shared his fate. We were then without a field officer, but the boys bore up bravely. They rallied 'round the flag and we advanced up the hill to find ourselves alone. It appears that the enemy broke through our lines off on our right, and word was sent to us on the left to fall back. Those in the rear of us received the order but the aide sent to us was shot before he reached us and so we got no orders. . . .

I returned to the fight, and our boys were dropping on all sides of me. I was blazing away at the rascals not ten rods off when a ball struck my gun just above the lower band as I was capping it, and cut it in two. The ball flew in pieces and part went by my head to the right and three pieces struck just below my left collarbone. The deepest

As though battles with bullets were not enough, brigades in winter quarters fought fiercely with snowballs.

one was not over half an inch, and stopping to open my coat I pulled them out and snatched a gun from Ames in Company H as he fell dead. Before I had fired this at all a ball clipped off a piece of the stock, and an instant after another struck the seam of my canteen and entered my left groin. I pulled it out, and, more maddened than ever, I rushed in again. A few minutes after, another ball took six inches off the muzzle of this gun. I snatched another from a wounded man under a tree, and, as I was loading, kneeling by the side of the road, a ball cut my rammer in two as I was turning it over my head. Another gun was easier got than a rammer so I threw that away and picked up a fourth one. Here in the road a buckshot struck me in the left eyebrow, making the third slight scratch I received in the action. It exceeded all I ever dreamed of, it was almost a miracle.

At South Mountain in 1862 McClellan's Union troops beat Lee's men in hand-to-hand fighting.

Then came the retreat across the river; rebels on three sides of us left no choice but to run or be killed or be taken prisoners. We left our all in the hollow by the creek and crossed the river to Smith's division. The bridge was torn up, and when I came to the river I threw my cartridge box on my shoulder and waded through. . . .

Sunday night we lay in a cornfield in the rain, without tent or blanket. Monday we went down on the James River, lying behind batteries to support them. Tuesday the same—six days exposed to a constant fire of shot and shell, till almost night, when we went to the front and engaged in another fierce conflict with the enemy. Going on to the field, I picked up a tent and slung it across my shoulder. The folds of that stopped a ball that would have passed through me. I picked it out, put it in my pocket, and, after firing sixty rounds of my own and a number of a wounded comrade's cartridges, I came off the field unhurt, and ready, but not anxious, for another fight.

From *Army Letters, 1861–1865*,
Oliver W. Norton, privately printed, 1903.

Thomas Livermore, a captain with the New Hampshire Infantry, recalls the battle of White Oak Swamp, another battle of that summer's campaign:

THE ENEMY'S FIRE was unremitting, and from noon until dark we endured the slow torture of seeing our comrades killed, mangled, and torn around us, while we could not fire a shot, as our business was to lie and wait to repel attacks and protect our batteries. With every discharge of the enemy's guns, the shells would scream over our heads and bury themselves in the woods beyond, burst over us and deal death in the ranks, or ricochet over the plain, killing whenever they struck a line. . . .

The shot hit some of our men and scattered their vitals and brains upon the ground, and we hugged the earth to escape this horrible fate, but nothing could save a few who fell victims there. I saw a shot strike in the 2d Delaware, a new regiment with us, which threw a man's head perhaps twenty feet into the air, and the bleeding trunk fell over toward us. The men seemed paralyzed for a moment, but presently gathered up the poor fellow's body in a blanket and carried it away. I do not know that I have ever feared artillery as I did then, and I can recollect very well how close I lay to the ground while the messengers of death, each one seemingly coming right into us, whistled over us. . . .

I had just reached my place when the order was given to rise up and face about. A cannon shot came quicker than the wind through my company, and close by me. Tibbetts fell and Nichols fell. We reached the line designated with a few hasty steps, and resumed our line with faces to the front. Nichols got up, and came back to the captain and said, "Captain, I am wounded and want to go to the rear." The poor fellow held up one arm with the other hand, for it dangled only by a strip of flesh. Some men went forward and hastily gathered up Tibbetts in a blanket and bore him away; the shot had gone through his body. We felt a little safer now. Hazzard's battery withdrew, cut to pieces, and with Captain Hazzard mortally wounded; and for a short time it seemed as if the rebels would fire unmolested, but Pettit galloped up with his

66

battery of 10-pounder Parrotts and went into action, and then iron did fly, and the rebels had their hands full. Captain Keller sat up on a knapsack in front of us and gave warning when the shells were coming, and perhaps saved lives by it; anyhow it was a brave thing to do.

From *Days and Events, 1860–1866*,
Thomas L. Livermore, Houghton Mifflin, 1920.

~~ 13 ~~

HUMAN NATURE ON THE RACK

In a second battle at Bull Run, in August 1862, the Federals were again defeated. Now Lee moved north, crossed the Potomac, and advanced into Maryland. McClellan met him in a bitter battle at Antietam. Several times during the long day it looked as if the Confederates would be overrun, but always they came back, and the day ended in a draw. The Union lost in killed and wounded about fourteen thousand men; the Confederates over eleven thousand.

David Thompson of the 9th New York Volunteers tells what he saw that day:

AS THE RANGE grew better, the firing became more rapid, the situation desperate and exasperating to the last degree. Human nature was on the rack, and there burst forth from

67

it the most vehement, terrible swearing I have ever heard. Certainly the joy of conflict was not ours that day. The suspense was only for a moment, however, for the order to charge came just after. Whether the regiment was thrown into disorder or not, I never knew. I only remember that as we rose and started, all the fire that had been held back so long was loosed. In a second the air was full of the hiss of bullets and the hurtle of grapeshot. . . . I see again, as I saw it then in a flash, a man just in front of me drop his musket and throw up his hands, stung into vigorous swearing by a bullet behind the ear. Many men fell going up the hill, but it seemed to be all over in a moment, and I found myself passing a hollow where a dozen wounded men lay—among them our sergeant-major, who was calling me to come down. He had caught sight of the blanket rolled across my back, and called me to unroll it and help to carry from the field one of our wounded lieutenants.

When I returned from obeying this summons the regiment was not to be seen. It had gone in on the run, what there was left of it, and had disappeared in the cornfield about the battery. There was nothing to do but lie there and await developments. Nearly all the men in the hollow were wounded, one man frightfully so, his arm being cut short off. He lived a few minutes only. All were calling for water, of course, but none was to be had.

We lay there till dusk, perhaps an hour, when the fighting ceased. During that hour, while the bullets snipped the leaves from a young locust tree growing at the edge of the hollow and powdered us with the fragments, we had time to speculate on many things—among others, on the impatience with which men clamor, in dull times, to be led into a fight. We heard all through the war that the army "was eager to be led against the enemy." It must have been so, for truthful correspondents said so, and editors confirmed it. But when you came to hunt for this particular itch, it was always the next regiment that had it. The truth is, when bullets are whacking against tree trunks and solid shot are cracking skulls like eggshells, the consuming passion in the breast of the average man is to get out of the way. Between the physical fear of going forward and the moral fear of turning back, there is a predicament of exceptional awkwardness from which a hidden hole in the ground would be a wonderfully welcome outlet.

Night fell, preventing further struggle. Of 600 men of the regiment who crossed the creek at 3 o'clock that afternoon, 45 were killed and 176 wounded. The Confederates held possession of that part of the field over which we had moved, and just after dusk they sent out detachments to collect arms and bring in prisoners. When they came to our hollow, all the unwounded and slightly wounded there were marched to the rear—prisoners of the 15th Georgia. We slept on the ground that night without protection of any kind; for, with a recklessness quite common throughout the war, we had thrown away every incumbrance on going into the fight.

From "With Burnside at Antietam," David I. Thompson, in *Battles and Leaders of the Civil War*, The Century Co., 1884–88.

Lincoln was dismayed when McClellan let Lee escape at Antietam. He replaced him with General Ambrose E. Burnside. Three months after Antietam, on December 13, Burnside's superior force was shattered at Fredericksburg in desperate assaults upon the Confederate position. Joshua L. Chamberlain, a colonel of the 20th Maine Volunteers, describes the sights and sounds of the battlefield when the firing ended:

THE DESPERATE CHARGE was over. We had not reached the enemy's fortifications, but only that fatal crest where we had seen five lines of battle mount but to be cut to earth as by a sword-swoop of fire. We have that costly honor which sometimes falls to the "reserve"—to go in when all is havoc and confusion, through storm and slaughter, to cover the broken and depleted. . . . Out of that silence from the battle's crash and roar rose new sounds more appalling still; rose or fell, you knew not which, or whether from the earth or air; a strange ventriloquism, of which you could not locate the source, a smothered moan that seemed to come from distances beyond reach of the natural sense, a wail so far and deep and wide, as if a thousand discords were flowing together into a keynote weird, unearthly, terrible to hear and bear, yet startling with its nearness; the writhing concord broken by cries for help, pierced by shrieks of paroxysm; some begging for a drop of water; some calling on God for pity; and some on friendly hands to finish what the enemy had so horribly begun; some with delirious, dreamy voices murmuring loved names, as if the dearest were bending over them; some gathering their last strength to fire a musket to call attention to them where they lay helpless and deserted; and underneath, all the time, that deep bass note from closed lips too hopeless or too heroic to articulate their agony. . . .

With a staff officer I sallied forth to see what we could do where the helpers seemed so few. Taking some observa-

70

An artist at the front captured the chaos in Fredericksburg when Union troops sacked the town following bombardment.

tions in order not to lose the bearing of our own position, we guided our steps by the most piteous of the cries. Our part was but little: to relieve a painful posture; to give a cooling draught to fevered lips; to compress a severed artery, as we had learned to do, though in bungling fashion; to apply a rude bandage, which yet might prolong the life to saving; to take a token or farewell message for some stricken home; it was but little, yet it was an endless task. We had moved towards the right and rear of our own position—the part of the field immediately above the city. The farther we went the more the need deepened, and the calls multiplied. Numbers half wakening from the lethargy of death, or of despair, by sounds of succor, begged us to take them quickly to a surgeon; and when we could not do that, imploring us to do the next most merciful service and give them quick dispatch out of their misery. Right glad were we when, after midnight, the shadowy ambulances came gliding along, and the kindly hospital stewards, with stretchers and soothing appliances, let us feel that we might return to our proper duty. . . .

The night chill had now woven a misty veil over the field. Except the few sentries along the front, the men had fallen asleep—the living with the dead. At last, outwearied and depressed with the desolate scene, my own strength sunk, and I moved two dead men a little and lay down between them, making a pillow of the breast of a third. The skirt of his overcoat drawn over my face helped also to shield me from the bleak winds. There was some comfort even in this companionship. But it was broken sleep. The deepening chill drove many forth to take the garments of those who could no longer need them, that they might keep themselves alive. More than once I was startled from my unrest by someone turning back the coat-skirt from my face, peering, half vampire-like, to my fancy, through the darkness to discover if it too were of the silent and unresisting; turning away more disconcerted at my living word than if a voice had spoken from the dead. . . .

From *Camp-Fire Sketches and Battle-Field Echoes*, W. C. King and W. P. Derby, eds., W. C. King & Co., 1887.

~⌒14⌒~

SLAVERY CHAIN DONE
BROKE AT LAST

*After the rout of the Union forces at Bull Run, the aboli-
tionists foresaw that the disaster would shock the North out
of its easy optimism and make it view the slavery issue in
another light. Blacks had all along said the issue was "freedom for all, or chains for all." Some abolitionists charged
that Lincoln was shortsighted, obstinate, slow to face up to
the necessity of emancipation. Why couldn't he see that
slavery was the cause of the war and only liberation of the
slaves would bring victory and end the war?*

*But as events proved, he moved deliberately in order to
mobilize the greatest number of Northerners behind the war
and to avoid driving away the border slave states. He knew
racism was rampant in the North; few soldiers wanted to
spill their blood to free the slave. Yet with every defeat
public feeling changed. What abolitionists feared was that
a peace might be patched out of compromise that would
leave slavery untouched. They knew presidential war power
was the one quick way to end slavery. So did Lincoln, and
when the tide began to turn in the Union's favor, he announced he would do it on January 1, 1863.*

*His decision transformed the war. Now it was a war to
preserve the Union and to end slavery. There would be no*

turning back, no compromise; it would be fought to the bitter end.

On January 1, throughout the North and in those parts of the South held by Union troops, crowds cheered as the words of the Emancipation Proclamation came over the wires, and yells rocketed into the air. In a jubilee meeting at a Union army camp in the South, the newly freed Blacks heard the magic words "forever free!" and suddenly began to sing:

My country, 'tis of thee,
Sweet land of liberty,
Of thee we sing!

Lincoln discussing emancipation of the slaves with his cabinet.

FREEDOM TO SLAVES!

Whereas, the President of the United States did, on the first day of the present month issue his Proclamation declaring "that, all persons held as Slaves in certain designated States, and parts of States, are, and henceforward shall be free," and that the Executive Government of the United States, including the Military and naval authorities thereof, would recognize and

Part of one of the many broadsides proclaiming issuance of the Emancipation Proclamation.

In Washington the Reverend Henry M. Turner, a free-born Black from South Carolina now living in the capital, watched his people greet the great news:

SEEING SUCH A multitude of people in and around my church, I hurriedly sent up to the office of the first paper in which the proclamation of freedom could be printed, known as the *Evening Star*, and squeezed myself through the dense crowd that was waiting for the paper. The first sheet run off with the proclamation in it was grabbed for by three of us, but some active young man got possession of it and fled. The next sheet was grabbed for by several, and was torn into tatters. The third sheet from the press was grabbed for by several, but I succeeded in procuring so much of it as contained the proclamation, and off I went for life and death. Down Pennsylvania Avenue I ran as for my life, and when the people saw me coming with the paper in my hand they raised a shouting cheer that was almost deafening. As many as could get around me lifted me to a great platform, and I started to read the proclamation. I had run the best end of a mile, I was out of breath,

75

and could not read. Mr. Hinton, to whom I handed the paper, read it with great force and clearness. While he was reading every kind of demonstration and gesticulation was going on. Men squealed, women fainted, dogs barked, white and colored people shook hands, songs were sung, and by this time cannons began to fire at the navy yard, and follow in the wake of the roar that had for some time been going on behind the White House. . . . Great processions of colored and white men marched to and fro and passed in front of the White House and congratulated President Lincoln on his proclamation. The President came to the window and made responsive bows, and thousands told him, if he would come out of that palace, they would hug him to death. . . . It was indeed a time of times, and nothing like it will ever be seen again in this life.

From *Marching Toward Freedom:*
The Negro in the Civil War, James McPherson, Knopf, 1965.

To Blacks everywhere emancipation meant the nation now had the chance to live up to the full implications of its democratic creed. That goal must be reached by burying the cruel heritage of racism and by accepting Blacks into full citizenship. Out of the black liberation came many songs that catch the passionate feeling of that great turning point. Here are two of them:

SLAVERY CHAIN

Slavery chain done broke at last,
Broke at last, broke at last,
Slavery chain done broke at last,
Going to praise God till I die.

76

Way down in-a dat valley,
Praying on my knees;
Told God about my troubles,
And to help me ef-a He please.

I did tell him how I suffer,
In de dungeon and de chain,
And de days I went with head bowed down,
And my broken flesh and pain.

Slavery chain done broke at last,
Broke at last, broke at last,
Slavery chain done broke at last,
Going to praise God till I die.

I did know my Jesus heard me,
'Cause de spirit spoke to me,
And said, "Rise my child, your chillun
And you too shall be free.

"I done 'p'int one mighty captain
For to marshall all my hosts,
And to bring my bleeding ones to me,
And not one shall be lost."

Slavery chain done broke at last,
Broke at last, broke at last,
Slavery chain done broke at last,
Going to praise God till I die.

NO MORE AUCTION BLOCK

No more auction block for me,
No more, no more,

No more auction block for me,
Many thousand gone.

No more peck of corn for me,
No more, no more,
No more peck of corn for me,
Many thousand gone.

No more pint of salt for me,
No more, no more,
No more pint of salt for me,
Many thousand gone.

No more driver's lash for me,
No more, no more,
No more driver's lash for me,
Many thousand gone.

From *The Negro Caravan*, Sterling A. Brown, ed., Citadel, 1941.

THE BLACK TROOPS
WERE HEROIC

From the sound of the first gun, Blacks had volunteered to fight. But Northern sentiment said no, you can't; this is "a white man's war." Frederick Douglass asked, "What on earth was the matter with the American government and

78

people? Do they really covet the world's ridicule as well as their own social and political ruin?" Ask the president, he said, "if this dark and terrible hour of the nation's extremity is a time for consulting a mere vulgar and unnatural prejudice. . . . This is no time to fight with one hand when both are needed. This is no time to fight with only your white hand, and allow your black hand to remain tied."

When given the chance, Blacks joined up eagerly. In the spring of 1862 a regiment of volunteers in South Carolina formed under the abolitionist General David Hunter, but after three months of service they were disbanded by government order. Another such group, formed by General Jim Lane in Kansas, suffered the same fate, though they saw action twice against Rebel guerrillas.

Finally, after the Emancipation Proclamation, Union ranks were opened to Blacks. But promises of equal treatment were not kept. Black servicemen suffered unequal pay, allowances, and opportunities throughout the war. Theirs was a two-sided fight: against slavery in the South and against discrimination in the North.

That they fought hard and well was soon proved to a doubting nation. This was just as true of freed slaves in the South who joined up as it was of Northern Blacks. The 2nd Louisiana, made up of ex-slaves, took part in the siege of Port Hudson, a key point in the campaign for control of the Mississippi. On May 27, 1863, a broad assault was made upon the fortifications. General Nathaniel P. Banks, in a letter to General H. W. Halleck in Washington, evaluated the performance of his black troops:

THE ARTILLERY opened fire between 5 and 6 o'clock, which was continued with animation during the day. At 10 o'clock Weitzel's brigade, with two regiments of col-

79

ored troops, made an assault upon the right of the enemy's works, crossing Sandy Creek, and driving them through the woods to their fortifications.

The fight lasted on this line until 4 o'clock, and was very severely contested. The enemy was driven into his works, and our troops moved up to the fortifications. On the extreme right of our line I posted the first and third regiments of Negro troops. The First Regiment of Louisiana Engineers, composed exclusively of colored men, excepting the officers, was also engaged in the operations of the day. The position occupied by these troops was one of importance, and called for the utmost steadiness and bravery in those to whom it was confided.

It gives me pleasure to report that they answered every expectation. Their conduct was heroic. No troops could be more determined or more daring. They made, during the day, three charges upon the batteries of the enemy, suffering very heavy losses, and holding their position at nightfall with the other troops on the right of our line. The highest commendation is bestowed upon them by all the officers in command on the right. Whatever doubt may have existed before as to the efficiency of organizations of this character, the history of this day proves conclusively to those who were in a condition to observe the conduct of these regiments, that the Government will find in this class of troops effective supporters and defenders.

The severe test to which they were subjected, and the determined manner in which they encountered the enemy, leave upon my mind no doubt of their ultimate success.

From *Washington and Jackson on Negro Soldiers*,
Henry C. Baird, ed., 1863.

A Union Army poster calling on black men to volunteer.

Ten days later, at Milliken's Bend, a small Louisiana town farther up the river, a bloody hand-to-hand fight took place between Rebel and Union forces. It was one of the bitterest struggles during a war famous for hard-fought actions. Three incomplete black regiments of ex-slaves from Louisiana and Mississippi were sent into the battle only sixteen days after they were mustered in. And thirty-nine percent of them were killed or wounded. "The bravery of the Blacks at Milliken's Bend," said Assistant Secretary of War Charles A. Dana, "completely revolutionized the sentiment of the army with regard to the employment of Negro troops."

81

Lincoln did not miss the lesson of Port Hudson and Milliken's Bend. He wrote out a message to be read at a public meeting in Springfield, Illinois:

I KNOW AS FULLY as anyone can know the opinions of others, that some of the commanders of our armies in the field, who have given us our most important successes, believe that the emancipation policy and the use of colored troops constitute the heaviest blow yet dealt to the rebellion, and that at least one of these important successes could not have been achieved when it was but for the aid of black soldiers. . . .

From *The Negro in the Civil War*,
Benjamin Quarles, Little, Brown, 1953.

By the war's end 180,000 Blacks had served in Lincoln's army and 30,000 in the navy, while 250,000 helped the military as laborers. To put an end to slavery, 38,000 Blacks gave their lives in battle. Twenty-one received the Congressional Medal of Honor. What they did helped to transform both the way the nation treated Blacks and the way Blacks saw themselves.

~16~

DRAFT RIOTS

Recruiting for the Union army was anything but fair or efficient. Early in March 1863 the Draft Law was adopted to guarantee more manpower. It made all men, ages twenty to forty-five, liable to military service. But it let any man with enough money hire a substitute to go in his place. This was grossly unfair to the poor, such as the Irish Americans, immigrants who worked hard and for low wages. The cities' Democratic press inflamed their sense of injustice by playing upon race prejudice. They cried that whites were being drafted to fight to free the hated "niggers," who would then come North to take their jobs at even lower pay.

When the first drawings for the draft began, riots broke out in many places—from New England to Wisconsin. In New York City riots raged in the streets for four days, July 13–16. The horrors of these riots were depicted by many witnesses. Anna Dickinson, an antislavery writer and lecturer, describes the attack upon a black orphanage:

LATE IN THE AFTERNOON a crowd which could have numbered not less than ten thousand, the majority of whom were ragged, frowzy, drunken women, gathered about the Orphan Asylum for Colored Children—a large and beautiful building and one of the most admirable and noble charities of the city. When it became evident from the menacing cries and groans of the multitude that danger, if not destruction, was meditated to the harmless and inoffensive inmates, a flag of truce appeared, and an appeal was made in their behalf, by the principal, to every sentiment of humanity which these beings might possess—a vain appeal! Whatever human feeling had ever, if ever, filled these souls was utterly drowned and washed away in the tide of rapine and blood in which they had been steeping themselves. The few officers who stood guard over the doors and manfully faced these demoniac legions were beaten down and flung to one side, helpless and stunned, whilst the vast crowd rushed in. All the articles upon which they could seize—beds, bedding, carpets, furniture, the very garments of the fleeing inmates, some of these torn from their persons as they sped by— were carried into the streets and hurried off by the women and children who stood ready to receive the goods which their husbands, sons, and fathers flung to their care.

The little ones, many of them assailed and beaten—all, orphans and caretakers, exposed to every indignity and every danger—driven on to the street, the building was fired. This had been attempted whilst the helpless children, some of them scarce more than babies, were still in their rooms; but this devilish consummation was prevented by the heroism of one man. He, the chief of the fire department, strove by voice and arm to stay the endeavor; and when, overcome by superior numbers, the brands had been lit and piled, with naked hands and in the face of threatened death he tore asunder the glowing embers and trod them underfoot. Again the effort was made and again failed through the determined and heroic opposition of this solitary soul. Then on the front steps, in the midst of these drunken and infuriated thousands, he stood up and besought them, if they cared nothing for themselves nor for those hapless orphans, that they would not bring lasting disgrace upon the city by destroying one of its noblest charities, which had for its object nothing but good.

Mobs rioting in New York against the draft law. A drugstore on Second Avenue is wrecked and looted, and a black man is lynched on Clarkson Street.

He was answered on all sides by yells and execrations and frenzied shrieks of "Down with the nagurs!" coupled with every oath and every curse that malignant hate of the blacks could devise and drunken Irish tongues could speak. It had been decreed that this building was to be razed to the ground. The house was fired in a thousand places, and in less than two hours the walls crashed in, a mass of smoking, blackened ruins, whilst the children wandered through the streets, a prey to beings who were wild beasts in everything save the superior ingenuity of man to agonize and torture his victims.

From *What Answer?*, Anna Dickinson, Ticknor, 1868.

The mobs roved over the city, seeking black victims everywhere. The Christian Recorder*'s man in Brooklyn reported what happened on that side of the river:*

MANY MEN were killed and thrown into rivers, a great number hung to trees and lampposts, numbers shot down; no black person could show their heads but what they were hunted like wolves. These scenes continued for four days. Hundreds of our people are in stationhouses, in the woods, and on Blackwell's Island. Over three thousand are today homeless and destitute, without means of support for their families. It is truly a day of distress to our race in this section. In Brooklyn we have not had any great trouble, but many of our people have been compelled to leave their houses and flee for refuge. The Irish have become so brutish that it is unsafe for families to live near them, and while I write, there are many now in the stations and country hiding from violence. . . .

In Weeksville and Flatbush, the colored men who had manhood in them armed themselves and threw out their pickets every day and night, determined to die defending their homes. Hundreds fled there from New York. . . . The mob spirit seemed to have run in every direction, and every little village catches the rebellious spirit. One instance is worthy of note. In the village of Flushing [Queens], the colored people went to the Catholic priest and told him that they were peaceable men doing no harm to anyone, and that the Irish had threatened to mob them, but if they did, they would burn two Irish houses for every one of theirs, and would kill two Irish men for every colored man killed by them. They were not mobbed, and so in every place where they were prepared they escaped being mobbed. Most of the colored men in Brooklyn who remained in the city were armed daily for self-defense.

From *Marching Toward Freedom*, McPherson, 1965.

A black family's home in Brooklyn was among the many besieged by the rioters. Maritcha Lyons, fifteen, told an investigating committee what happened:

ON THE AFTERNOON of July [13] a rabble attacked our house, breaking windowpanes, smashing shutters and partially demolishing the front door. Before dusk arrangements had been effected to secure the safety of the children. As the evening drew on, a resolute man and a courageous woman quietly seated themselves in the hall, determined to sell their lives as dearly as may be. Just after midnight a second mob was gathering. As one of the

87

rioters attempted to ascend the front steps, Father advanced into the doorway and fired point-blank into the crowd. The mob retreated and no further demonstration was made that night. The next day a third and successful attempt at entrance was effected. This sent Father over the back fence while Mother took refuge on the premises of a neighbor.

In one short hour, the police cleared the premises. What a home! Its interior was dismantled, furniture was missing or broken. From basement to attic evidences of vandalism prevailed. A fire, kindled in one of the upper rooms, was discovered in time to prevent a conflagration. Under cover of darkness the police conveyed our parents to the Williamsburg ferry. Mother with her children undertook the hazardous journey to New England. We reached Salem tired, travel-stained, with only the garments we had on.

From *We Are Your Sisters: Black Women in the Nineteenth Century*, Dorothy Sterling, ed., Norton, 1984.

~~ 17 ~~

MONITOR VERSUS
MERRIMAC

As soon as the war began Lincoln blockaded the whole coast of the Confederacy. And to the South's despair, foreign governments respected the blockade. The North's naval task was heavy: to close off a dozen major ports and some two hundred minor ones, and this with only twenty vessels. But Union shipyards got busy and by war's end had built six hundred ships. One port after another was captured or sealed off as the blockade grew steadily tighter. The Confederacy built ships too, and bought others from England to serve as raiders on the high seas. But the Federal blockade was never overcome, and it strangled the South's economy.

The most famous sea battle was fought on March 9, 1862, between the Rebel Merrimac and the Union's Monitor. The Merrimac was a big ironclad ship covered with armor plate, and in its first fights it easily destroyed two of the Union's wooden ships. The Union then built a metalclad ship of its own, the Monitor. A small vessel, it lay low in the water and had a revolving gun turret.

The five-hour fight, the first between ironclads, ended in a draw. It is described by Lieutenant William F. Keeler, the Monitor's acting paymaster:

89

As a light fog lifted from the water it revealed the *Merrimac* with her consorts lying under Sewall's Point. The announcement of breakfast brought also the news that the *Merrimac* was coming, and our coffee was forgotten. . . .

Everyone on board of us was at his post, except the doctor and myself, who having no place assigned us in the immediate working of the ship were making the most of our time in taking a good look at our still distant but approaching foe. A puff of smoke arose from her side and a shell howled over our heads. Capt. Worden, who was on deck, came up and said more sternly than I ever heard him speak before, "Gentlemen, that is the *Merrimac*, you had better go below."

We did not wait [for] a second invitation but ascended the tower and down the hatchway, Capt. W. following. The iron hatch was closed over the opening and all access to us cut off. As we passed down through the turret the gunners were lifting a 175 lb. shot into the mouth of one of our immense guns. "Send them that with our compliments, my lads," says Capt. W.

A few straggling rays of light found their way from the top of the tower to the depths below which was dimly lighted by lanterns. Everyone was at his post, fixed like a statue; the most profound silence reigned—if there had been a coward heart there its throb would have been audible, so intense was the stillness.

I experienced a peculiar sensation; I do not think it was fear, but it was different from anything I ever knew before. We were enclosed in what we supposed to be an impenetrable armor—we knew that a powerful foe was about to meet us—ours was an untried experiment and our enemy's first fire might make it a coffin for us all.

Then we knew not how soon the attack would commence, or from what direction it would come, for with the exception of those in the pilothouse and one or two in the turret, no one of us could see her. The suspense was awful as we waited in the dim light expecting every moment to hear the crash of our enemy's shot.

Soon came the report of a gun, then another and another at short intervals, then a rapid discharge. Then a thundering broadside and the infernal howl (I can't give it a more appropriate name) of the shells as they flew over our vessel was all that broke the silence and made it seem still more terrible.

Mr. Green says, "Paymaster, ask the Capt. if I shall fire." The reply was, "Tell Mr. Green not to fire till I give the word, to be cool and deliberate, to take sure aim and not waste a shot."

O, what a relief it was, when at the word, the gun over my head thundered out its challenge with a report which jarred our vessel, but it was music to us all. . . . Until we fired, the *Merrimac* had taken no notice of us, confining her attentions to the *Minnesota*. Our second shot struck her and made the iron scales rattle on her side. She seemed for the first time to be aware of our presence and replied to our solid shot with grape and canister which rattled on our iron decks like hailstones.

One of the gunners in the turret could not resist the temptation when the port was open for an instant to run out his head; he drew it in with a broad grin. "Well," says he, "the d——d fools are firing canister at us."

The same silence was [again] enforced below that no order might be lost or misunderstood.

The vessels were now sufficiently near to make our fire effective, and our two heavy pieces were worked as rapidly as possible, every shot telling—the intervals being filled by the howling of the shells around and over us, which was now incessant.

The men at the guns had stripped themselves to their waists and were covered with powder and smoke, the perspiration falling from them like rain.

Below, we had no idea of the position of our unseen antagonist, her mode of attack, or her distance from us, except what was made known through the orders of the Capt. . . .

The sounds of the conflict at this time were terrible. The rapid firing of our own guns amid the clouds of smoke . . . mingled with the crash of solid shot against our sides and the bursting of shells all around us. Two men had been sent down from the turret, who were knocked senseless by balls striking the outside of the turret while they happened to be in contact with the inside. . . .

At this time a heavy shell struck the pilothouse—I was standing near, waiting an order, heard the report which was unusually heavy, a flash of light and a cloud of smoke filled the house. I noticed the Capt. stagger and put his hands to his eyes—I ran up to him and asked if he was hurt.

"My eyes," says he. "I am blind."

With the assistance of the surgeon I got him down and called Lieut. Green from the turret. A number of us collected around him; the blood was running from his face, which was blackened with the powder smoke. He said, "Gentlemen, I leave it with you, do what you think best. I cannot see, but do not mind me."

The *Monitor* and *Merrimac* meet in a sea battle.

The quartermaster at the wheel, as soon as Capt. W. was hurt, had turned from our antagonist and we were now some distance from her. We held a hurried consultation and "fight" was the unanimous voice of all.

Lieut. Green took Capt. W.'s position and our bow was again pointed for the *Merrimac*. As we neared her she seemed inclined to haul off and after a few more guns on each side, Mr. Green gave the order to stop firing as she was out of range and hauling off. We did not pursue as we were anxious to relieve Capt. W. and have more done for him than could be done aboard.

Our iron hatches were slid back and we sprang out on deck, which was strewn with fragments of the fight. Our foe gave us a shell as a parting fire which shrieked just over our heads and exploded about 100 feet beyond us.

From *Aboard the U.S.* Monitor: *1862*, Robert W. Daly, ed., United States Naval Institute Press 1964.

──○ 18 ○──

TURNING POINT AT
GETTYSBURG

General Lee decided to carry the war into the North's terri-
tory, this time into Pennsylvania. His hope was to gain
foreign recognition of the Confederacy by winning a major
battle and, at the same time, to encourage defeatism in the
North. His army met General George Gordon Meade's
army at Gettysburg. The small town became the scene of
the biggest battle ever fought in North America.

On July 2 and 3, 1863, the two armies stood facing each
other across a valley. Lee sent his men against the Union
positions in a series of bold attacks. But Meade's soldiers
stood solid and would not be dislodged. Meade, the stronger
by fifteen thousand troops, had greater firepower and a
good defensive position.

The first day's fighting saw action by a famous artillery
brigade of Meade's army. Augustus Buell, known as the
"boy cannoneer," recalls years later what it was like:

HOW THOSE peerless cannoneers sprang to their work! . . .
The very guns became things of life—not implements, but
comrades. Every man was doing the work of two or three.
At our gun at the finish there were only the Corporal,
No. 1 and No. 3, with two drivers fetching ammunition.
The water in Pat's bucket was like ink. His face and hands
were smeared all over with burnt powder. The thumbstall

of No. 3 was burned to a crisp by the hot vent field. Between the black of the burnt powder and the crimson streaks from his bloody head, Packard looked like a demon from below! Up and down the line men reeling and falling; splinters flying from wheels and axles where bullets hit; in rear, horses tearing and plunging, mad with wounds of terror; drivers yelling, shells bursting, shot shrieking overhead, howling about our ears or throwing up great clouds of dust where they struck; the musketry crashing on three sides of us; bullets hissing, humming and whistling everywhere; cannon roaring; all crash on crash and peal on peal, smoke, dust, splinters, blood, wreck and carnage indescribable; but the brass guns of Old B still bellowed and not a man or boy flinched or faltered! Every

As Lee's army invaded Pennsylvania, posters went up warning of the great danger and calling the militia to defend the Union.

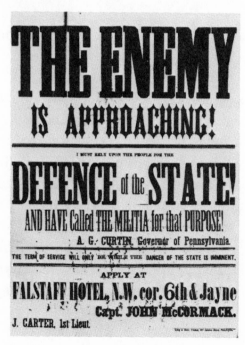

man's shirt soaked with sweat and many of them sopped with blood from wounds not severe enough to make such bulldogs "let go"—bareheaded, sleeves rolled up, faces blackened—oh! if such a picture could be spread on canvas to the life! Out in front of us an undulating field, filled almost as far as the eye could reach with a long, low, gray line creeping toward us, fairly fringed with flame! . . .

From "Recollections of Service in the Army of the Potomac,"
Augustus Buell, in *The National Tribune*, 1890.

The hills held by the Union were heavily defended, and when Lee failed to coordinate his attacks, he lost great numbers of men, and the Confederates were forced to retreat. One of Lee's young soldiers, Randolph McKim, remembers the defeat of that day:

THEN CAME General Ewell's order to assume the offensive and assail the crest of Culp's Hill, on our right. . . . The works to be stormed ran almost at right angles to those we occupied. Moreover, there was a double line of entrenchments, one above the other, and each filled with troops. In moving to the attack we were exposed to enfilading fire from the woods on our left flank, besides the double line of fire which we had to face in front, and a battery of artillery posted on a hill to our left rear opened upon us at short range. . . .

On swept the gallant little brigade, the Third North Carolina on the right of the line, next the Second Maryland, then the three Virginia regiments (10th, 23d, and

37th), with the First North Carolina on the extreme left. Its ranks had been sadly thinned, and its energies greatly depleted by those six fearful hours of battle that morning; but its nerve and spirit were undiminished. Soon, however, the left and center were checked and then repulsed, probably by the severe flank fire from the woods; and the small remnant of the Third North Carolina, with the stronger Second Maryland (I do not recall the banners of any other regiment), were far in advance of the rest of the line. On they pressed to within about twenty or thirty paces of the works—a small but gallant band of heroes daring to attempt what could not be done by flesh and blood.

The end soon came. We were beaten back to the line from which we had advanced with terrible loss, and in much confusion, but the enemy did not make a counter-charge. By the strenuous efforts of the officers of the line and of the staff, order was restored, and we re-formed in the breastworks from which we had emerged, there to be again exposed to an artillery fire exceeding in violence that of the early morning. It remains only to say that, like Pickett's men later in the day, this single brigade was hurled unsupported against the enemy's works. Daniel's brigade remained in the breastworks during and after the charge, and neither from that command nor from any other had we any support. Of course it is to be presumed that General Daniel acted in obedience to orders. We remained in this breastwork after the charge about an hour before we finally abandoned the Federal entrenchments and retired to the foot of the hill.

From *A Soldier's Recollections: Leaves from the Diary of a Young Confederate*, Randolph McKim, Longmans, Green, 1910.

His role in the second day at Gettysburg, July 3, was set down by Abner Small, who was with the Union regiment sacrificed to cover the last withdrawal of troops from Seminary Ridge:

NOON CAME, and the sun blazed fiercely hot, and the silence fretted us. Time was counted through minutes that seemed hours and an hour that seemed an eternity. Then away down the Emmitsburg road a rebel cannon flashed, and a puff of smoke blew and hung on the still summer air; then another; and then from all the rebel line there was one vast roar, and a storm of screaming metal swept across the valley. Our guns blazed and thundered in reply. The earth groaned and trembled. The air, thick with smoke and sulphurous vapor, almost suffocated the troops in support of the batteries. Through the murk we heard hoarse commands, the bursting of shells, cries of agony. We saw caissons hit and blown up, splinters flying, men flung to the ground, horses torn and shrieking. Solid shot hit the hill in our front, sprayed battalions with fountains of dirt, and went plunging into the ranks, crushing flesh and bone. Under that awful fire, continuous, relentless, our brigade and all our line held tight and unfaltering.

About two o'clock our brigade was moved from the left to the right of the cemetery and placed in support of batteries there. How that short march was made, I don't know. The air was all murderous iron; it seemed as if there couldn't be room for any soldier upright and in motion. We stayed an hour in our new position, exposed not only to shelling from both east and west, but also to the galling fire of rebel skirmishers. . . .

About three o'clock we were again moved to the left,

from the hill to the ridge. Many of the Union guns were now ceasing their fire; damaged batteries were going to the rear, and others were hurrying up from the reserve. Shot and shell from the enemy still pounded the hill. The ground was strewn with dead horses. Here and there were dead men. We wondered, as we passed through the cemetery, that we weren't smashed into the earth to mingle with mouldering citizens of peace.

As we hastened toward the ridge we heard a thunder of artillery there, and musketry that wasn't the crash of volleys or the harsh rattle of scattered firing, but one continuous din. The long-awaited assault had come. As we topped the ridge we caught another tone of the uproar, strange and terrible; a sound that came from thousands of human throats, yet was not a commingling of shouts and yells, but rather like a vast mournful roar. Down the slope in front of us the ground was strewn with soldiers in every conceivable vehemence of action, and agony, and death. Men in gray, surrounded and overwhelmed, were throwing up their hands in surrender. Others were falling back into the valley. Many were lying in the trampled fields, dying and dead. The assault had failed. I felt pity for the victims of that ruined hope. Looking down on the scene of their defeat and of our victory, I could only see a square mile of Tophet.

Our brigade moved forward as the enemy fell back, and we took part in a general skirmish fire that was kept up by both sides until after dark. We threw up breastworks; and when it was learned, about eleven o'clock, that the rebels in our front were taking down fences, perhaps to clear the way for another attack, we strengthened our works with rails from fences within our reach. The brigade

Yankee artillery placed on the heights smash the Confederate attack at Gettysburg.

was busy with this labor almost all night.

July 4th the armies kept their opposing lines all day without attacking or being attacked. Skirmishing continued. The morning was lowery, and some rain fell, and shortly after noon there came a drenching downpour and a wild wind. The wounded lying on the ground, and protected only by trees, were in a sorry plight. All the wounded along our front had been brought in by the morning of this day, and were being cared for by medical officers with ordinary supplies; but the trains had not come up yet, and the field hospital could provide little shelter.

My duties permitting, I went among the wounded in a grove on the left of our position, where lay many hurt survivors of the rebel attacking force; men of Pickett's division, and Heth's, and Pender's. I proffered what assistance I could. I remember stopping beside one poor fellow who was shot through the body. His wants were few. "Only a drink of water. I'm cold; so cold. Won't you cover me up?" Then his mind wandered, and he murmured something about his mother. Then he had a clear sense of his condition. Would I write to his home, and say how he loved them, and how he died? "Tell them all about it, won't you? Father's name is Robert Jenkins. My name is Will." I thought I heard him say that he belonged to the 7th North Carolina and came from Chatham County. His words faltered into silence. I covered his face. . . .

From *The Road to Richmond: The Civil War Memoirs of Major Abner R. Small*, Harold Adams Small, ed., University of California Press, 1957.

Reluctant to admit defeat, Lee lingered, waiting the next day for a Union attack. But the battle had cost Meade twenty-five thousand casualties and he let Lee alone. (The Confederate casualties totaled twenty-eight thousand.) Late on July 4 Lee headed his army toward the Potomac under a soaking rain. One of his men, Napier Bartlett, of the Louisiana Artillery, describes the mood of the retreat:

THE DAY ALTOGETHER was productive of different emotions from any ever experienced on any other battlefield. The sight of the dying and wounded who were lying by the thousand between the two lines, and compelled amid their sufferings to witness and be exposed to the cannonade of over 200 guns, and later in the day, the reckless charges, and the subsequent destruction or demoralization of Lee's best corps—the fury, tears or savage irony of the commanders—the patient waiting, which would occasionally

101

break out into sardonic laughter at the ruin of our hopes seen everywhere around us, and finally, the decisive moment, when the enemy seemed to be launching his cavalry to sweep the remaining handful of men from the face of the earth: These were all incidents which settled, and will forever remain in the memory. We all remember Gettysburg, though we do not remember and do not care to remember many other of the remaining incidents of the war. . . .

But to return to the battlefield, from which at a little distance we bivouacked that night. It is true that many of us shed tears at the way in which our dreams of liberty had ended, and then and there gave them a much more careful burial than most of the dead received; yet when we were permitted at length to lie down under the caissons, or in the fence corners, and realized that we had escaped the death that had snatched away so many others, we felt too well satisfied at our good fortune—in spite of the enemy still near us, not to sleep the soundest sleep it is permitted on earth for mortals to enjoy. . . .

Never had the men and horses been so jaded, and stove up. One of our men who dropped at the foot of a tree in a sort of hollow, went to sleep, and continued sleeping until the water rose to his waist. It was only then that he could be awakened with the greatest difficulty. Battery horses would drop down dead. So important was our movement that no halt for bivouac, though we marched scarcely two miles an hour, was made during the route from Gettysburg to Williamsport—a march of over 40 miles. The men and officers on horseback would go to sleep without knowing it, and at one time there was a halt occasioned by all of the drivers—or at least those whose business was to attend to it, being asleep in their saddles. In fact the whole of the army was dozing while marching and moved as if under enchantment or a spell—were asleep and at the same time walking.

From *A Soldier's Story of the War*, Napier Bartlett, 1874.

19

THAT THESE DEAD SHALL NOT HAVE DIED IN VAIN

About four months after the battle, on November 19, 1863, the military cemetery at Gettysburg was dedicated. The principal address was given by the country's most popular orator, Edward Everett—clergyman, writer, diplomat, once president of Harvard University, secretary of state, and U.S. senator. He talked for two hours, not uncommon in those days.

Then Lincoln stood up. He had been invited to attend, and was casually asked to say just a few words after Mr. Everett. He read to the crowd these three brief paragraphs, now considered to be one of the finest examples of great writing in the English language. Though reprinted (and memorized) countless times, they are still worth reading yet another time:

103

FOURSCORE AND seven years ago our fathers brought forth on this continent a new nation, conceived in Liberty and dedicated to the proposition that all men are created equal.

Now we are engaged in a great civil war, testing whether that nation, or any nation so conceived and so dedicated, can long endure. We are met on a great battle-field of that war. We have come to dedicate a portion of that field, as a final resting-place for those who here gave their lives that that nation might live. It is altogether fitting and proper that we should do this.

But, in a larger sense, we can not dedicate—we can not consecrate—we can not hallow—this ground. The brave men, living and dead, who struggled here, have conse-crated it, far above our poor power to add or detract. The world will little note, nor long remember, what we say here, but it can never forget what they did here. It is for us the living, rather, to be dedicated here to the unfinished work which they who fought here have thus far so nobly advanced. It is rather for us to be here dedicated to the great task remaining before us—that from these honored dead we take increased devotion to that cause for which they gave the last full measure of devotion—that we here highly resolve that these dead shall not have died in vain— that this nation, under God, shall have a new birth of freedom—and that government of the people, by the peo-ple, for the people, shall not perish from the earth.

From *The Collected Works of Abraham Lincoln*, Roy P. Basler, ed., Rutgers University Press, 1953.

The
Gettysburg Address

The second draft of the Gettysburg
Address, from which Lincoln read
his enduring words. Note that
he seems to have made word
changes at the last minute and that
the final version of the address differs in
some details from the spoken address.

~⌒ 20 ⌒~

ON THE HOME FRONT

*With the war more than half over, the Union victory seem-
ing more likely, what was happening on the home front? For
the North it was a boom time. Production swelled, prices
shot up, and profits with them. Wages, however, rose by only
a third as much as prices. Though two million men would
serve in the Union's armed forces, that loss of manpower
was made up by three developments. Immigrants flooded
in, almost 800,000 during the war years; new technology
saved labor on farms and in factories; and women seized the
job openings as men went off to fight or quit old jobs for
better ones. Teaching school is one example: It paid so little
that men quit and women replaced them at even lower
salaries. By the thousands women moved into government
and industrial jobs, to be terribly exploited. They protested,
organized, struck for better conditions. They made the
myth of the helpless woman look ridiculous.*

*Evidence of women's work for the war was gathered by
Mary Livermore, a social reformer who volunteered for the
Sanitary Commission in the Midwest. As she moved about
collecting vast amounts of fruits and vegetables to help the
Union army overcome the disease called scurvy, she saw
what women could do:*

IN THE EARLY SUMMER of 1863, frequent calls of business took me through the extensive farming districts of

Wisconsin, and Eastern Iowa, when the farmers were the busiest, gathering the wheat harvest. As we dashed along the railway, let our course lead in whatever direction it might, it took us through what seemed a continuous wheat field. The yellow grain was waving everywhere; and two-horse reapers were cutting it down in a whole-sale fashion that would have astonished Eastern farmers. Hundreds of reapers could be counted in a ride of half a dozen hours. . . .

Women were in the field everywhere, driving the reap-ers, binding and shocking, and loading grain, until then an unusual sight. At first, it displeased me, and I turned away in aversion. By and by, I observed how skillfully they drove the horses around and around the wheat field, di-minishing more and more its periphery at every circuit, the glittering blades of the reaper cutting wide swaths with a rapid, clicking sound that was pleasant to hear. Then I saw that when they followed the reapers, binding and shocking, although they did not keep up with the men, their work was done with more precision and nicety, and their sheaves had an artistic finish that those lacked made by the men. So I said to myself, "They are worthy women, and deserve praise: their husbands are probably too poor to hire help, and, like the 'helpmeets' God designed them to be, they have girt themselves to this work—and they are doing it superbly. Good wives! Good women!"

One day my route took me off the railway, some twenty miles across the country. But we drove through the same golden fields of grain, and between great stretches of green waving corn. Now a river shimmered like silver through the gold of the wheat and oats, and now a growth of young timber made a dark green background for the harvest

107

Women working at a munitions plant in Watertown, Massachusetts.

fields. Here, as everywhere, women were busy at the harvesting. . . .

I stepped over where the girls were binding the fallen grain. They were fine, well-built lasses, with the honest eyes and firm mouth of the mother, brown like her, and clad in the same sensible costume.

"Well, you are like your mother, not afraid to lend a hand at the harvesting, it seems!" was my opening remark.

"No, we're willing to help outdoors in these times. Harvesting isn't any harder, if it's as hard as cooking, washing, and ironing, over a red-hot stove in July and August— only we have to do both now. My three brothers went into the army, all my cousins, most of the young men about here, and the men we used to hire. So there's no help to be got but women, and the crops must be got in all the same, you know."

From *My Story of the War*, Mary A. Livermore, Worthington, 1888.

In the South too women substituted for men in many jobs, and ran the farms when their men left for the front. White manpower was short, of course, but slave productivity helped make up for the loss. With each year, growing shortages of food and factory products made life harsher. People starved in many places.

A daily record of hardship in the Confederate capital at Richmond was kept by John B. Jones, a clerk in Jefferson Davis's War Department:

MAY 23, 1862—Oh, the extortioners! Meats of all kinds are selling at fifty cents per pound; butter, seventy-five cents; coffee, a dollar and half; tea, ten dollars; boots, thirty dollars per pair; shoes, eighteen dollars; ladies' shoes, fifteen dollars; shirts, six dollars each. Houses that rented for five hundred dollars last year are a thousand dollars now. Boarding, from thirty to forty dollars per month. General Winder has issued an order fixing the maximum prices of certain articles of marketing, which has only the effect of keeping a great many things out of market. The farmers have to pay . . . extortionate prices and complain very justly of the partiality of the general. It does more harm than good.

OCTOBER 1ST—How shall we subsist this winter? There is not a supply of wood or coal in the city—and it is said that there are not adequate means of transporting it hither. Flour at sixteen dollars per barrel and bacon at seventy-five cents per pound threaten a famine. And yet there are no beggars in the streets. We must get a million of men in arms and drive the invader from our soil. We are capable of it, and we must do it. Better die in battle than die of starvation produced by the enemy. . . .

DECEMBER 1ST—God speed the day of peace! Our patriotism is mainly in the army and among the ladies of the South. The avarice and cupidity of the men at home could only be excelled by the ravenous wolves; and most of our sufferings are fully deserved. Where a people will not have mercy on one another, how can they expect mercy? They depreciate the Confederate notes by charging from $20 to $40 per bbl. for flour; $3.50 per bushel of meal, $2 per lb. for butter; $20 per cord for wood, etc. When we shall have peace let the extortionists be remembered! Let an indelible stigma be branded upon them.

A portion of the people look like vagabonds. We see men and women and children in the streets in dingy and dilapidated clothes; and some seem gaunt and pale with hunger—the speculators and thieving quartermasters and commissaries only looking sleek and comfortable. If this state of things continues a year or so longer, they will have their reward. There will be governmental bankruptcy, and all their gains will turn to dust and ashes, dust and ashes! . . .

OCTOBER 22ND, 1863—A poor woman yesterday applied to a merchant in Carey Street to purchase a barrel of flour. The price he demanded was $70.

"My God!" exclaimed she, "how can I pay such prices? I have seven children; what shall I do?"

"I don't know, madam," said he, coolly, "unless you eat your children."

Such is the power of cupidity—it transforms men into

110

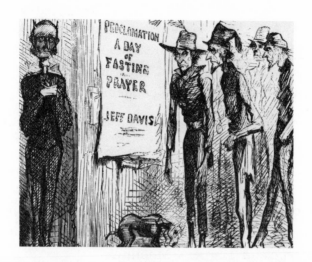

Life on the Confederate home front became grimmer as the war wore on, and many suffered great hunger. This Northern cartoon pokes fun at the proclamation of fasting posted by Jefferson Davis, depicted at left as a horned devil.

Southern women join in a bread riot at Richmond to protest profiteering.

demons. And if this spirit prevails throughout the country, a just God will bring calamities upon the land, which will reach these cormorants, but which, it may be feared, will involve all classes in a common ruin.

From *A Rebel War Clerk's Diary at the Confederate States Capital*, John B. Jones, Lippincott, 1866.

"The battle of Bull Run," said one leading financier of the war years, "makes the fortune of every man in Wall Street who is not an idiot." How speculation ran riot is told in an article in Harper's Monthly:

PAPER MONEY brought everyone into Wall Street, and interested every family in the ups and downs of stocks. It circulated like fertilizing dew throughout the land, generating enterprise, facilitating industry, developing internal trade; the railways found their business increase beyond their most sanguine expectations; dividend-paying roads had extra profits to divide; embarrassed enterprises cleared off their debts and became lucrative to their owners; everybody wanted to own railway property. . . .

It is keeping within bounds to say that $250,000,000—in paper money—was realized as profits by the operators in stocks between 1862 and 1864. The difference between the aggregate price of the railroad and miscellaneous shares and bonds dealt in on our Stock Exchange at midsummer, 1862, and the price of the same securities on 1st August, 1864, is more than that sum. Many popular shares rose 300 percent.

This profit was divided among many thousands of people. In 1863, and in the first quarter of 1864, everybody

112

seemed to be speculating in stocks. Nothing else was talked of at clubs, in the streets, at the theaters, in drawing rooms. Ladies privately pledged their diamonds as margin with brokers, and astonished their husbands with the display of their gains. Clergymen staked their salary, and some of them realized in a few months more than they could have made by a lifetime of preaching. One man, who had nothing in the world but a horse, sent him to a broker's stable, and persuaded the broker to buy him a hundred shares; he drew from the broker, a few months after, a balance of $300,000. . . .

The labors and profits of the brokers were enormous. One house checked more than once for $4,000,000 in a day. A day's commissions, in the case of a leading firm, were not infrequently $5,000. Nearly all the leading members of the board lost their voices from constant brawling, and talked in the evening as though they were in the last stage of bronchitis; clerks seldom left their offices before 11 or 12 P.M., a liberal dinner at Delmonico's being allowed by their employers as a stimulus to exertion. The day was not long enough for the gamblers. . . .

From "Wall Street in War Time," *Harper's Monthly*, April 1865.

To make a fortune quickly and easily in wartime was not enough for the profiteers. They hastened to spend their wealth in lavish display. The New York Herald *called it the "Age of Shoddy":*

ALL OUR THEATERS are open . . . and they are all crowded nightly. The kind of entertainment given seems to be of little account. Provided the prices are high and the place

113

fashionable nothing more is required. All the hotels are as crowded as the theaters; and it is noticeable that the most costly accommodations, in both hotels and theaters, are the first and most eagerly taken. Our merchants report the same phenomenon in their stores: the richest silks, laces, and jewelry are the soonest sold. At least five hundred new turnouts may be seen any fine afternoon in the park; and neither Rotten Row, London, nor the Bois de Boulogne, Paris, can show a more splendid sight. Before the golden days of the Indian summer are over these five hundred new equipages will be increased to a thousand. Not to keep a carriage, not to wear diamonds, not to be attired in a robe which cost a small fortune, is now equivalent to being a nobody.

This war has entirely changed the American character. The lavish profusion in which the old Southern cotton aristocracy used to indulge is completely eclipsed by the dash, parade, and magnificence of the new Northern shoddy aristocracy of this period. Ideas of cheapness and economy are thrown to the winds. The individual who makes the most money—no matter how—and spends the most money—no matter for what—is considered the greatest man. To be extravagant is to be fashionable. These facts sufficiently account for the immense and brilliant audiences at the opera and the theaters; and until the final crash comes such audiences will undoubtedly continue.

The world has seen its iron age, its silver age, its golden age and its brazen age. This is the age of shoddy. The new brownstone palaces on Fifth Avenue, the new equipages at the park, the new diamonds which dazzle unaccustomed eyes, the new silks and satins which rustle over

114

Wall Street speculators who made fat profits out of the war were accused of fraud and forgery.

loudly, as if to demand attention, the new people who live in the palaces and ride in the carriages and wear the diamonds and silks—all are shoddy. From the devil's dust they sprang and unto the devil's dust they shall return. They live in shoddy houses. They ride in shoddy carriages, drawn by shoddy horses, and driven by shoddy coachmen who wear shoddy liveries. They lie upon shoddy beds, which have just come from the upholsterer's and still smell of shoddy varnish. They wear shoddy clothes purchased from shoddy merchants, who have erected mammoth stores, which appear to be marble, but are really shoddy. They set or follow the shoddy fashions, and fondly imagine themselves a la mode de Paris, when they are only a la mode de shoddy.

Their professions and occupations are pure shoddy. They are shoddy brokers in Wall Street, or shoddy manu-

115

facturers of shoddy goods, or shoddy contractors for shoddy articles for a shoddy government. Six days in a week they are shoddy businessmen. On the seventh day they are shoddy Christians. They ride luxuriously to a shoddy church, where a shoddy clergyman reads to them from a shoddy Bible and preaches a shoddy sermon written upon gilt-edged paper; and, during the appropriate passages, this shoddy successor to the old Apostles wipes his weak eyes with a shoddy lace handkerchief as he mildly pleads with his hearers, who are sleeping soundly upon their shoddy cushions, and begs of them to believe that the Savior was crucified with intolerable torments in order that the shoddy aristocracy might be gently wafted upon the wings of shoddy angels to a shoddy heaven.

Nor are their politics less shoddy than their religion. They belong to the shoddy party, which is always loyal to shoddy, and they vote the shoddy ticket and support the shoddy administration which is conducting this shoddy war, not for the obsolete idea of the restoration of the Union, but for the profit and perpetuation of a shoddy dynasty. Oh, for some Junius, with a pen as keen as shoddy steel and words that burn like shoddy "Greek fire," to write the history of this shoddy age, and prophesy that downfall of shoddy which is to come! Already shrewd Daniels scent a storm in the Babylonish air; but still the days are golden and King Shoddy marches on triumphantly. Let us, then, enjoy the present, the park, the theaters and the opera, and leave the future to take care of itself. That is the sum of shoddy wisdom, and we shall not question such high authority.

From the *New York Herald*, October 6, 1863.

116

Not everyone was rich, or even middle-class. The vast majority were poor. In the cities they lived in slum tenements, more than half of them occupied by immigrant families. Did anyone care about the extent of poverty, the neglect of the misery, the depth of suffering? New York City's Council of Hygiene and Public Health made a report on slum conditions in 1865, the last year of the war:

IN SOME OF the apartments of the tenant-houses the rags that cover the floor in lieu of a carpet reek with filth. They have become a receptacle for street mud, food of all kinds, saliva, urine, and faeces. . . . The bed clothing is often little better. . . .

That the evils and abuses of the system continue undiminished is seen on every hand. Not only does filth, overcrowding, lack of privacy and domesticity, lack of ventilation and lighting, and absence of supervision and of sanitary regulation, still characterize the greater number of them; but they are built to a greater height in stories, there are more rear tenant-houses erected back to back with other buildings, correspondingly situated on parallel streets; the courts and alleys are more greedily encroached upon and narrowed into unventilated, unlighted, damp, and well-like holes between the many-storied front and rear tenements; and more fever-breeding . . . culs-de-sac are created as the demand for the humble homes of the laboring poor increases. . . .

It is not our purpose to present unnecessary details upon this subject, but simply to state what nuisances are to be regarded as injurious to public health and to individual welfare in our city. They may be enumerated as follows: (1) filthy streets; (2) neglected garbage and domestic refuse; (3) obstructed and faulty sewers and drains; (4) neglected privies and stables; (5) cattle pens and large stables in the more populous districts; (6) neglected and filthy markets; (7) slaughterhouses and hide and fat depots in close proximity to populous streets; (8) droves of cattle and swine in crowded streets; (9) swill-milk stables and their products; (10) bone boiling, fat melting, and their accompaniments within the city limits; (11) the sulphuretted, ammoniacal, and carburetted gases and offensive exhalations that are needlessly liberated and widely diffused in gas manufacture and purification; (12) the accumulations of dumping grounds and manure yards in vicinity of populous streets; (13) the present management of refuse and junk materials in the city; (14) the unreasonable overcrowding of the city railway cars, and the absence of all sanitary authority, permitting the unguarded transit and public exposure of persons with smallpox and other loathsome maladies in the public conveyances and otherwise in the streets; (15) the neglect of dead animals in the streets and the gutters of the city.

From *Report of Council of Hygiene and Public Health Upon the Sanitary Condition of the City,* Appleton, 1865.

~~ 21 ~~
DEATH FOR DESERTERS

No disease is as destructive to an army, someone once said, as laxity of discipline. Yet Americans have never been quick to accept discipline. Everyone feels he is the equal of all the others, no matter his station in life—"Who is he to give me orders?" It was hard enough to get Americans to respect the civil law; military law was totally foreign to all but a handful of professional soldiers. It took a long time to drive home to huge armies of raw recruits the value of rules and discipline.

What made it worse was the way both Federal and Confederate armies were officered. At the top on both sides was a small number of trained and experienced commanding officers. But most of the field officers were appointed by politicians, and lower officers were elected by the rank and file. Few of them knew anything about the rules of warfare or the need for discipline.

So discipline in general was weak in the first years of the war. It got better as the officer corps learned the hard way and got rid of the incompetents, and of course, as the troops became used to military life. While discipline improved, lapses in many groups and places were frequent and sometimes crippled even a whole army. Discipline was poorest where troops were distant from the battleground and given little to do. That happened often in the first two years. Active fighting was sporadic; close fighting lasted only a

119

short time, and then there were long periods of idleness while the men recovered, reorganized, and waited, waited, waited.

Discipline was good when leadership was good. That was vital to morale. Even within the same regiment one well-officered company might be much superior to another with poor leadership.

The result of weak discipline was widespread refusal to take orders and a terribly high rate of desertion. (The Union army recorded over 260,000 desertions.) Punishment for breach of discipline varied markedly. Officers could be harsh or lenient, authoritative or feeble, respected or despised.

Private John Haley of the 17th Maine Regiment kept a journal of his life in the Union army. In these passages he notes the punishment given deserters:

JANUARY 6TH, 1863—The division was paraded to witness the reward meted out to privates whose "precarious pegs" have too good an opinion of them to stand by and see their body abused. When an officer's legs are thus shaky, they are frequently braced by promotion, and if this doesn't work he is allowed to resign under some specious plea such as ill health or pressing claims.

Francis Hermon of the 1st New York was the individual suspected of desertion. He was marched 'round three sides of a square of soldiers to impress on them the enormity of his crime. His head was shaved and he was escorted out of camp to the tune of the "Rogue's March." "He deserted his comrades in the face of the enemy," says the record. This youth belonged to that regiment placed in rear of us to keep us from running. He wasn't the only

120

guilty one, but they couldn't drum out the entire regiment.

The Maine troops thus far have had no love for the particular tune and its accompanying exercises: shaved heads, branded hips, and a procession with bayonets at their heels. The New Yorkers have different tastes, and the "Rogue's March" is sweeter music to them than the whistle of bullets or the screaming of shells. Perhaps we shall have the same feelings when we have been in the show as long and have endured as much as they. . . .

JANUARY 19TH—Paraded again to witness another highly elevating exhibition. A man from the 37th New York had his head shaved and a C, for coward, branded on his hip. Branding a human being like a pork barrel is a relic of barbarism. Before the curtain rose on this scene, an order

Desertion from both armies was so widespread that harsh measures were taken to stop it. Here a deserter labeled "Coward" is drummed out of the Union ranks.

was promulgated saying we "must not express any approbation or disapprobation at anything we might witness today." Several disregarded this injunction and expressed their disgust at these proceedings and their contempt for the executors. Any commander who thinks we would honor such a display is ignorant of the American character! We haven't lost quite all our sense of decency, nor our courage to rebuke such uncivilized spectacles.

DECEMBER 5TH–FEBRUARY 5, 1864—Nothing of importance has occurred for some time except the execution of a private from the 4th Maine "for cowardice in the presence of the enemy." Doubtless there are cases of desertion so glaringly aggravating that they should be dealt with summarily, but no man should be shot like a dog for cowardice, this not being a matter within the control of the individual. Some will, I'm sure, urge that a coward of this type shouldn't enlist. This would be good logic if it could be shown that all men know themselves. But they do not. Men are moved by great popular currents, and enthusiasm of this kind is often mistaken for courage. We cannot judge men by the mere fact of enlistment. They are honest and patriotic and no doubt meant to do all they enlisted to do, but it is one thing to talk about "staring Death out of countenance," and quite another to do it. Alas for human calculations, they so often miscarry.

From *The Rebel Yell and the Yankee Hurrah:
The Civil War Journal of a Maine Volunteer*, Down East Books, 1985

*Desertions in the Confederate army were high, too,
though no figures are available. Many Confederates went*

122

off without leave to visit their families nearby or to help get in the crops. On both sides huge numbers evaded the draft and were never caught. Some Confederate deserters, especially those from the border states, favored the Union and fled into its lines when the chance came. But not many Federal troops deserted to the Rebel side. Although the penalty for desertion was death, only a small percentage of the guilty were executed.

In this extract from a letter to a friend, Washington Gardner, serving with General Philip Sheridan's Union troops, describes the execution of two deserters at Chattanooga in November 1863:

I WITNESSED a painful sight this afternoon—the shooting of two federal soldiers. . . . The two men belonged to Illinois regiments: one to the 44th and the other to the 88th, both of our division, which as you know is commanded by General Sheridan. The men had been tried for desertion, found guilty and sentenced to be shot. One brigade of the division under arms, with colors flying and band playing, formed about noon in nearly a hollow square with one side entirely open. Thousands of soldier spectators gathered about those who stood under arms. About one P.M. a solemn procession composed of two details of infantry, one in front of the prisoners and one in the rear, marched into the inclosure. Behind the first company and immediately in front of the prisoners their coffins were borne, each upon the shoulders of four men. In the rear of the doomed men marched the second company with their rifles at the right shoulder shift and bayonets fixed. A band playing a solemn tune marched with slow and measured step in front of the little procession.

123

General Sheridan and staff were present. All were mounted and all in full uniform. The General had a broad yellow sash over his shoulder drawn across his breast and down under his sword belt. He sat motionless upon his big black horse, which stood just a little in front of the other horsemen. When the procession arrived at the open side of the square it was halted, the coffins were placed upon the ground, when the prisoners knelt and the chaplain prayed. They then arose, apparently very calm, and sat erect, each upon his coffin. A bandage was then bound over the eyes of each. A platoon of soldiers with loaded rifles stood a few paces in front. There was a strange silence for a moment and then the voice of command rang out. "Ready!" "Aim!" "Fire!" And each of the prisoners fell back over his coffin, dead.

It was hard to see men thus killed by their own comrades but you have no idea how many have deserted, encouraged by friends at home to do the disgraceful act. Sad as the scene this afternoon was, it will have a wholesome effect upon the whole division.

From "Civil War Letters of Washington Gardner,"
Michigan History Magazine, I, 1917.

Writing home to his wife, the Confederate surgeon Spencer Welch, of the 13th South Carolina Volunteers, tells of his reaction to executions he witnessed:

SEPTEMBER 27, 1863—Camp near Orange Court House, Va.,—We had nine more military executions in our division yesterday—one man from Thomas' Brigade, one

124

from Scales' and seven from Lane's. Colonel Hunt was a member of the court-martial which sentenced them, and he tells me that one of the men from Lane's Brigade was a brother of your preacher, and that the two looked very much alike. He said he was a very intelligent man, and gave as his reason for deserting that the editorials in the Raleigh *Standard* had convinced him that Jeff Davis was a tyrant and that the Confederate cause was wrong. I am surprised that the editor of that miserable little journal is allowed to go at large. It is most unfortunate that this thing of shooting men for desertion was not begun sooner. Many lives would have been saved by it, because a great many men will now have to be shot before the trouble can be stopped. . . .

From *A Confederate Surgeon's Letters to His Wife*,
Spencer G. Welch, Neale, 1911.

NEVER TO DESTROY LIFE

For pacifists the Civil War posed a deeply troubling question. Most of them, North or South, detested slavery. What to do about their convictions now? As pacifists they opposed war because they believed it destroys life, corrupts society, violates morality. No matter what the cause of any war, absolute pacifists refuse to have any part in it—not only the fighting, but also paying taxes or equipping troops or doing labor. Others this time were willing to accept some kinds of alternative service so long as they were not forced to fight. And still others, such as many young Quakers, were willing to fight for the Union because they opposed slavery so strongly and believed this war would liberate the slaves. When the two values they cherished most came into opposition, they chose the one above the other.

The religious peace sects—Mennonites, Shakers, Amish, Seventh-Day Adventists, and others—were the staunchest in upholding their principles. John Kline, an elder of the Church of the Brethren, was a native of Virginia. In a letter to a prominent officer he appealed to the Confederates on behalf of men forced into the ranks despite their conscientious scruples against military service:

WE GERMAN BAPTISTS (called Tunkers) do most solemnly believe that the bearing of carnal weapons in order to destroy life is in direct opposition to the Gospel of Christ, which we accept as the rule of our faith and practice. To this we have most solemnly vowed to be true until death. Hence we stand pledged to our God to carry out that which we believe to be his commandment. . . . We feel bound to pay our taxes, fines, and to do whatever is in our power which does not conflict with our obligation to God. . . . But in this unholy contest, both law and all former precedents of making drafts have been set aside. The privilege usually granted Christian people to pay a fine has been overruled and set aside, and they are compelled to take up weapons of car-

126

nal warfare. This is not only revolting to them, but a positive violation to their solemn vow to their God. This is without precedent in a land of Christian liberty. Who the prosecutor of this outrage on our constitutional rights is I know not, but that it is so is clear. . . .

This state of things the much abused Abe Lincoln would have much deplored. For I am credibly informed that he issued a proclamation that no conscientious Christian should be forced to war or to take up arms. Thus it should be in a land of Christian liberty. None but those who have a disposition or desire to rear up a hierarchy or despotic government could feel otherwise. None that have the spirit of Washington or Jefferson in their hearts would desire to compel their fellow countrymen to take up arms against their conscience, and to force them to kill their fellow man. . . . A great breach of the constitution has been practiced on us for we have been enforced, restrained and molested because of our religious belief and opinion. Please give this matter your earnest attention and tell it or read it to your fellow officers. . . .

From *Pacifism in the United States*, Peter Brock, Princeton, 1968.

Some among the Amish and Mennonites who had been drafted into the Union army agreed to pay an exemption fee to get out of service, while others paid for a substitute. But their churches disapproved of their actions. Bishop Jacob Schwarzendruber of Iowa told his fellow Amish:

CONCERNING THE DRAFT, or buying volunteer substitutes or paying volunteers to send them out to fight, I hold that it is wrong according to God's Word and the teaching of

127

Jesus and the apostles, as it has been in our congregations. And I hold that it is a guilt upon us ministers and the church. . . . The Saviour's teaching is not as we have done, that we should be permitted to buy substitutes or help to pay for people and let them go to kill others. . . . Do I then pay someone to do injustice?

From *Pacifism in the United States*, Brock, 1968.

Utopian communities, antislavery in conviction, nevertheless rejected all war, including this one. But trying to show their neighbors they were still good and loyal citizens, they issued such statements as this one from the Hopedale Community in Massachusetts:

THOUGH WE HAVE no moral sympathy whatever with the insurrectionists, but much with the Federal government and its loyal adherents; and though we see that the loyalists, on their own worldly plane of moral action, must conquer the rebels by overwhelming deadly force, or ignominiously abandon their constitutional government, and falsify their solemn obligations of allegiance; yet we feel nonetheless bound to abide with Christ on his high

Mennonite homes in Kansas, where many pacifists who resisted service in the Civil War came from.

plane of peaceful righteousness, and thereby endeavor, however gradually, to leaven the minds of mankind with those benignant principles which alone can put an end to all disorder and violence.

From *Pacifism in the United States*, Brock, 1968.

～ 23 ～

IS THIS HELL?

Whether you were a Federal or Confederate soldier, to be captured and confined in a prisoner-of-war camp was dreaded by all. Neither side was prepared for a long war, or anticipated the care of vast numbers of prisoners. Both North and South improvised to meet the necessity, using empty factories and warehouses and civil jails, or throwing up immense open stockades. Exchange of prisoners, though agreed upon, was seldom carried out. Prison conditions were abominable—overcrowding; little or bad food, clothing, shelter; and wretched medical and sanitary provisions. Each side took around 200,000 prisoners, with about one seventh of them dying in captivity.

The most notorious prison was at Andersonville in Georgia, though conditions in some Northern prisons were reported to be just as terrible. Andersonville began taking in captured Federal soldiers early in 1864. By the war's end 50,000 men, all privates, had suffered its horrors, with a third of them dying. Prescott Tracy of the 82nd Regiment, the New York Volunteers, survived the prison to give this testimony:

ON ENTERING THE Stockade Prison, we found it crowded with twenty-eight thousand of our fellow soldiers. By crowded, I mean that it was difficult to move in any direction without jostling and being jostled. This prison is an open space, twenty-five acres, without trees or shelter of any kind. The soil is sand over a bottom of clay. The fence is made of upright trunks of trees, about twenty feet high, near the top of which are small platforms, where the guards are stationed. Twenty feet inside and parallel to the fence is a light railing, forming the "dead line," beyond which the projection of a foot or finger is sure to bring the deadly bullet of the sentinel.

Through the ground creeps a stream five to six feet in width, the water about ankle deep, and near the middle of the enclosure spreading out into a swamp of about six acres, filled with refuse wood, stumps and debris of the camp. Before entering this enclosure, the stream, or more properly sewer, passes through the camp of the guards, receiving from this source, and others farther up, a large amount of the vilest material, even the contents of the sink. The water is of a dark color, and an ordinary glass would collect a thick sediment. This was our only drinking and cooking water. It was our custom to filter it as best we could through our remnants of haversacks, shirts and blouses. Wells had been dug, but the water either proved so productive of diarrhea, or so limited in quantity, that

130

they were of no general use. The cookhouse was situated on the stream just outside the stockade, and its refuse of decaying offal was thrown into the water, a greasy coating covering much of the surface. To these was added the daily large amount of base matter from the camp itself. There was a system of policing, but the means was so limited, and so large a number of the men was rendered irresolute and depressed by imprisonment, that the work was very imperfectly done. One side of the swamp was naturally used as a sink, the men usually going out some distance into the water. Under the summer sun this place early became corruption too vile for description, the men breeding disgusting life, so that the surface of the water moved as with a gentle breeze.

The newcomers, on reaching this, would exclaim: "Is this hell?" yet they soon would become callous, and enter unmoved the horrible rottenness. The rebel authorities never removed any filth. We were never permitted to go outside, except at times, in small squads, to gather our firewood. During the building of the cookhouse, a few, who were carpenters, were ordered out to assist.

Our only shelter from the sun and rain and night dews was what we could make by stretching over us our coats or scraps of blankets, which a few had, but generally there was no attempt by day or night to protect ourselves.

The rations consisted of eight ounces of corn bread (the cob being ground with the kernel) and, generally sour, two ounces of condemned pork, offensive in appearance and smell. Occasionally, about twice a week, two tablespoons of rice, and in place of the pork the same amount (two tablespoonfuls) of molasses were given us about twice a month. To the best of my knowledge, information and belief, our ration was in quality a starving one, it being either too foul to be touched or too raw to be digested. We never had a supply of wood. I have often seen men with a little bag of meal in hand, gathered from several rations, starving to death for want of wood, and in desperation would mix the raw material with water and try to eat it.

The clothing of the men was miserable in the extreme. Very few had shoes of any kind, not two thousand had coats and pants, and those were latecomers. More than one half were indecently exposed, and many were naked.

The usual punishment was to place the men in the stocks, outside, near the Captain's quarters. If a man was missing at roll call, the squad of ninety to which he belonged was deprived of the ration. The "dead-line" bullet, already referred to, spared no offender. About two a day were thus shot, some being cases of suicide, brought on by mental depression or physical misery, the poor fellows throwing themselves, or madly rushing, outside the "line."

The mental condition of a large portion of the men was melancholy, beginning in despondency and tending to a kind of stolid and idiotic indifference. Many spent much time in arousing and encouraging their fellows, but hundreds were lying about motionless, or stalking vacantly to and fro, quite beyond any help which could be given them within their prison walls. These cases were frequent among those who had been imprisoned but a short time. . . .

The proportion of deaths from starvation, not including those consequent on the diseases originating in the character and limited quantity of food, such as diarrhea, dysentery and scurvy, I cannot state; but to the best of my

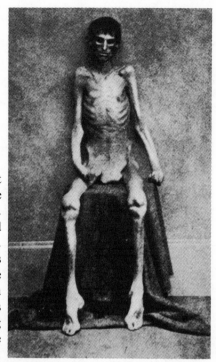

Many Union prisoners at Andersonville, a Confederate camp, starved to death. This photograph shocked the country. But conditions in Federal camps could be terrible too. In the sketch below, Confederate prisoners are punished by a killing stretch of time astride a sawhorse.

knowledge, information and belief, there were scores every month. We could, at any time, point out many for which such a fate was inevitable, as they lay or feebly walked, mere skeletons. . . . In some cases the inner edges of the two bones of the arms, between the elbow and the wrist, with the intermediate blood vessels, were plainly visible when held toward the light. The ration, in quantity, was perhaps barely sufficient to sustain life, and the cases of starvation were generally those whose stomachs could not retain what had become entirely indigestible.

For a man to find, on waking, that his comrade by his side was dead, was an occurrence too common to be noted. I have seen death in almost all the forms of the hospital and battlefield, but the daily scenes exceeded in the extremity of misery all my previous experience.

From *Narrative of the Privations and Suffering of United States Officers and Privates While Prisoners of War in the Hands of Rebel Authorities.*

24

TO WORK, NOT TO WEEP

Disease took more victims in the Civil War than the bullet did, and the toll from both was enormous. In the Federal forces four men died of sickness for every one killed in battle. In the early period almost one out of every four soldiers fell sick. It was just as bad or worse for the Confederates. At least half the men in a regiment could not fight for sickness, and often more. One authority on Confederate medicine estimated that on the average each Southern soldier was sick or wounded six times during the war. But five times as many fell sick as were injured.

In both armies one reason illness was rampant was because the authorities failed to sift out the unfit at induction. The physical examination of recruits was a joke. But the chief reason for so much disease was medicine's ignorance of its cause. Doctors knew nothing about "germs." Bacteriology did not yet exist. Medicines were few. Sanitation was crude. Troops drank water from any source, however contaminated it might be. Camps were set up in swamps, drainage was poor, tents were placed too closely together. Latrines—often just uncovered narrow trenches—not only made the area stink but also made the men sick. The list of causes runs on: neglect of personal cleanliness, bad garbage disposal, poor clothing and shelter, exposure to all kinds of weather. Dysentery and diarrhea were the most common of camp diseases, and after them came malaria

Although many women on both sides volunteered as nurses in army hospitals, they were often harassed by the military and medical officers.

and typhoid and pneumonia and scurvy and much more.

Perhaps as great a handicap as ignorance were the inadequate hospital facilities for both armies, and the poorly organized medical staffs. This multiplied the miseries of the wounded and the sick. Each battle produced a flood of casualties that swamped hospitals always short of doctors and nurses and medicines.

One of those who volunteered to nurse was Louisa May Alcott (later to write Little Women *and other popular novels for children). She reported for duty to a Washington hospital late in 1862, but soon was invalided home with typhoid fever. She writes about her intense experiences shortly after:*

THERE THEY WERE! "Our brave boys," as the papers justly call them, for cowards could hardly have been so riddled with shot and shell, so torn and shattered, nor have borne suffering for which we have no name, with an uncomplaining fortitude, which made one glad to cherish each as a brother. In they came, some on stretchers, some in men's arms, some feebly staggering along propped on rude crutches, and one lay stark and still with covered face, as a comrade gave his name to be recorded before they carried him away to the dead house. All was hurry and confusion; the hall was full of these wrecks of humanity, for the most exhausted could not reach a bed till duly ticketed and registered; the walls were lined with rows of such as could sit, the floor covered with the more disabled, the steps and doorways filled with helpers and lookers-on; the sound of many feet and voices made that usually quiet hour as noisy as noon; and, in the midst of it all, the matron's motherly face brought more comfort to many a poor soul than the cordial draughts she administered, or the cheery words that welcomed all, making of the hospital a home.

(The sight of several stretchers, each with its legless, armless, or desperately wounded occupant, entering my ward, admonished me that I was there to work, not to wonder or weep; so I corked up my feelings, and returned to the path of duty, which was rather "a hard road to travel" just then.) (The house had been a hotel before hospitals were needed, and many of the doors still bore their old names; some not so inappropriate as might be imagined, for my ward was in truth a ball-room, if gunshot wounds could christen it.) Forty beds were prepared, many already tenanted by tired men who fell down anywhere, and drowsed till the smell of food roused them. Round the great stove was gathered the dreariest group I ever saw—ragged, gaunt and pale, mud to the knees, with bloody bandages untouched since put on days before; many bundled up in blankets, coats being lost or useless; and all wearing that disheartened look which proclaimed defeat more plainly than any telegram of the Burnside blunder. I pitied them so much, I dared not speak to them, though, remembering all they had been through since the rout at Fredericksburg, I yearned to serve the dreariest of them all. Presently, Miss Blank tore me from my refuge behind piles of one-sleeved shirts, odd socks, bandages and lint; put basin, sponge, towels, and a block of brown soap into my hands, with these appalling directions:

"Come, my dear, begin to wash as fast as you can. Tell them to take off socks, coats and shirts, scrub them well, put on clean shirts, and the attendants will finish them off, and lay them in bed."

If she had requested me to shave them all, or dance a hornpipe on the stove funnel, I should have been less staggered; but to scrub some dozen lords of creation at a moment's notice, was really—really—. However, there was no time for nonsense, and, having resolved when I came to do everything I was bid, I drowned my scruples in my washbowl, clutched my soap manfully, and, assuming a businesslike air, made a dab at the first dirty specimen I saw, bent on performing my task *vi et armis* [by strength and by arms] if necessary. I chanced to light on a withered old Irishman, wounded in the head, which caused that portion of his frame to be tastefully laid out like a garden, the bandages being the walks, his hair the shrubbery. He was so overpowered by the honor of having a lady wash him, as he expressed it, that he did nothing but roll up his eyes, and bless me, in an irresistible style

138

which was too much for my sense of the ludicrous; so we laughed together, and when I knelt down to take off his shoes, he "flopped" also and wouldn't hear of my touching "them dirty craters. May your bed above be aisy darlin', for the day's work ye are doon!—Woosh! There ye are, and bedad, it's hard tellin' which is the dirtiest, the fut or the shoe." It was; and if he hadn't been to the fore, I should have gone on pulling, under the impression that the "fut" was a boot, for trousers, socks, shoes and legs, were a mass of mud. This comical tableau produced a general grin, at which propitious beginning I took heart and scrubbed away like any tidy parent on a Saturday night. Some of them took the performance like sleepy children, leaning their tired heads against me as I worked, others looked grimly scandalized, and several of the roughest colored like bashful girls. One wore a soiled little bag about his neck, and, as I moved it, to bathe his wounded breast, I said,

"Your talisman didn't save you, did it?"

"Well, I reckon it did, marm, for that shot would a gone a couple a inches deeper but for my old mammy's camphor bag," answered the cheerful philosopher.

Another, with a gunshot wound through the cheek, asked for a looking glass, and when I brought one, regarded his swollen face with a dolorous expression, as he muttered—

"I vow to gosh, that's too bad! I warn't a bad-looking chap before, and now I'm done for; won't there be a thunderin' scar? And what on earth will Josephine Skinner say?"

From *Hospital Sketches*, Louisa May Alcott, 1863.

139

Walt Whitman, the great poet who had written Leaves
of Grass, *volunteered as a male nurse in 1862. He cared
for both Union and Confederate wounded in field hospitals
at the front and in hospitals in Washington. His wartime
journal expresses the suffering of the soldiers he ministered
to and his own sad feelings about the national tragedy of
such a war:*

THURSDAY, JAN. 21, 1863—Devoted the main part of the
day to Armory-square hospital; went pretty thoroughly
through wards F, G, H, and I; some fifty cases in each
ward. In ward F supplied the men throughout with writing paper and stamp'd envelope each; distributed in small
portions, to proper subjects, a large jar of first-rate pre-
serv'd berries, which had been donated to me by a lady—
her own cooking. Found several cases I thought good
subjects for small sums of money, which I furnish'd. (The
wounded men often come up broke, and it helps their
spirits to have even the small sum I give them.) My paper
and envelopes all gone, but distributed a good lot of amusing reading matter; also, as I thought judicious, tobacco,
oranges, apples, etc. Interesting cases in Ward I; Charles
Miller, bed 19, company D, 53d Pennsylvania, is only
sixteen years of age, very bright, courageous boy, left leg
amputated below the knee; next bed to him, another
young lad very sick; gave each appropriate gifts. In the bed
above, also, amputation of the left leg; gave him a little jar
of raspberries; bed one, this ward, gave a small sum; also
to a soldier on crutches, sitting on his bed near . . . (I am
more and more surprised at the very great proportion of
youngsters from fifteen to twenty-one in the army. I after-

140

Battlefront surgery was brutal: the saw, and a swig of liquor to ease the pain.

wards found a still greater proportion among the southerners.)

Evening, same day, went to see D.F.R., before alluded to; found him remarkably changed for the better; up and dress'd—quite a triumph; he afterwards got well, and went back to his regiment. Distributed in the wards a quantity of note-paper, and forty or fifty stamp'd envelopes, of which I had recruited my stock, and the men were much in need. . . .

When eligible, I encourage the men to write, and myself, when called upon, write all sorts of letters for them (including love letters, very tender ones). Almost as I reel off these memoranda, I write for a new patient to his wife, M. de F., of the 17th Connecticut, company H, has just come up (February 17th) from Windmill Point, and is received in ward H, Armory-square. He is an intelligent-looking man, has a foreign accent, black-eyed and hair'd, a Hebraic appearance. Wants a telegraphic message sent to his wife, New Canaan, Conn. I agree to send the message—but to make things sure I also sit down and write the wife a letter, and despatch it to the post office immediately, as he fears she will come on, and he does not wish her to, as he will surely get well. . . .

FEBRUARY 23—I must not let the great hospital at the Patent Office pass away without some mention. A few weeks ago the vast area of the second story of that noblest of Washington buildings was crowded close with rows of sick, badly wounded and dying soldiers. They were placed in three very large apartments. I went there many times. It was a strange, solemn, and, with all its features of suffering and death, a sort of fascinating sight. I go some-

142

times at night to soothe and relieve particular cases. Two of the immense apartments are fill'd with high and ponderous glass cases, crowded with models in miniature of every kind of utensil, machine or invention it ever enter'd into the mind of man to conceive; and with curiosities and foreign presents. Between these cases are lateral openings, perhaps eight feet wide and quite deep, and in these were placed the sick, besides a great long double row of them up and down through the middle of the hall. Many of them were very bad cases, wounds and amputations. Then there was a gallery running above the hall in which there were beds also. It was, indeed, a curious scene, especially at night when lit up. The glass cases, the beds, the forms lying there, the gallery above, and the marble pavement underfoot—the suffering, and the fortitude to bear it in various degrees—occasionally, from some the groan that could not be repress'd—sometimes a poor fellow dying, with emaciated face and glassy eye, the nurse by his side, the doctor also there, but no friend, no relative. . . .

From *Walt Whitman, Specimen Days and Collect*, Rees Welch, 1882–83.

During the Peninsular campaign the Union army used ships to move the wounded from the field to hospitals. Katharine Wormeley, a volunteer for the Sanitary Commission, a private relief organization, served on the Daniel Webster No. 2 *transport. In June 1862 she wrote her mother about what she did when several hundred wounded men were carried aboard the transport:*

WE WENT ON BOARD; and such a scene as we entered and lived in for two days I trust never to see again. Men in

143

every condition of horror, shattered and shrieking, were being brought in on stretchers borne by "contrabands," who dumped them anywhere, banged the stretchers against pillars and posts, and walked over the men without compassion. There was no one to direct what ward or what bed they were to go into. Men shattered in the thigh, and even cases of amputation, were shoveled into top berths without thought or mercy. The men had mostly been without food for three days, but there was nothing on board for them; and if there had been, the cooks were only engaged to cook for the ship, and not for the hospital.

We began to do what we could. The first thing wanted by wounded men is something to drink (with the sick, stimulants are the first thing). Fortunately we had plenty of lemons, ice, and sherry on board, and these were available at once. Dr. Ware discovered a barrel of molasses, which, with vinegar, ice, and water, made a most refreshing drink. After that we gave them crackers and milk, or tea and bread. It was hopeless to try to get them into bed; indeed, there were no mattresses. All we could do at first was to try to calm the confusion, to stop some agony, to revive the fainting lives, to snatch, if possible, from immediate death with food and stimulants. Imagine a great river or sound steamer filled on every deck—every berth and every square inch of room covered with wounded men; even the stairs and gangways and guards filled with those who are less badly wounded; and then imagine fifty well men, on every kind of errand, rushing to and fro over them, every touch bringing agony to the poor fellows, while stretcher after stretcher came along, hoping to find an empty place; and then imagine what it was to keep calm ourselves, and make sure that every man on both boats

144

was properly refreshed and fed. We got through about one
A.M. . . .

From *The Other Side of the War; With the Army of the Potomac,*
Katharine Wormeley, Ticknor, 1889.

*In the South, the Women's Relief Society was formed to
collect funds and provide aid for sick and wounded soldiers.
Susan Lee Blackford, a Virginian, was one of the thousands
of Southern women who volunteered for nursing duty. She
tells of her experience nursing wounded Confederates at
Lynchburg in this letter of May 12, 1864:*

MAY 12TH—My writing desk has been open all day, yet
I have just found time to write to you. Mrs. Spence came
after me just as I was about to begin this morning and said
she had just heard that the Taliaferro's factory was full of
soldiers in a deplorable condition. I went down there with
a bucket of rice milk, a basin, towel, soap, etc. to see what
I could do. I found the house filled with wounded men and
not one thing provided for them. They were lying about
the floor on a little straw. Some had been there since
Tuesday and had not seen a surgeon. I washed and dressed
the wounds of about fifty and poured water over the
wounds of many more. The town is crowded with the poor
creatures, and there is really no preparations for such a
number. If it had not been for the ladies many of them
would have starved to death. The poor creatures are very
grateful, and it is a great pleasure to us to help them in any
way. I have been hard at work ever since the wounded
commenced coming. I went to the depot twice to see what
I could do. I have had the cutting and distribution of

145

twelve hundred yards of cotton cloth for bandages, and sent over three bushels of rolls of bandages, and as many more yesterday. I have never worked so hard in all my life and I would rather do that than anything else in the world. I hope no more wounded are sent here as I really do not think they could be sheltered. The doctors, of course, are doing much, and some are doing their full duty, but the majority are not. They have free access to the hospital stores and deem their own health demands that they drink up most the brandy and whiskey in stock, and, being fired up most of the time, display a cruel and brutal indifference to the needs of the suffering, which is a disgrace to their profession and to humanity.

From *Letters from Lee's Army*, Susan Lee Blackford, Scribner's, 1947.

∼⌒25⌒∼

THE KILLING OF STRANGERS

The most decisive battlegrounds of the war were in the East, but the fighting in the West influenced the final outcome. It was a region rich in men and supplies; whoever controlled it might possibly tip the balance in the East. Missouri, a slave state, became the cockpit of struggle for domination. Many of its people were Southerners, and the state govern-

ment was in their hands. It seemed likely that it would line up with the Confederates or fall to an invasion by their troops. Fighting broke out at once, and for over two years the outcome was uncertain.

As the war began, one Missourian who would become a world-famous writer was working on the Mississippi as a riverboat pilot. His brother pilots debated which side to join in the war. Mark Twain, then twenty-four, couldn't make up his mind. He went home to Hannibal to think about it. What happened next he told in this fictionally embroidered account of his brief Civil War experience. It is a mixture of the comic adventures of a Confederate irregular with a dark, dreamlike view of war's horror:

. . . IN THAT SUMMER—of 1861—the first wash of the wave of war broke upon the shores of Missouri. Our State was invaded by the Union forces. They took possession of St. Louis, Jefferson Barracks, and some other points. The Governor, Claib Jackson, issued his proclamation calling out fifty thousand militia to repel the invader.

I was visiting in the small town where my boyhood had been spent—Hannibal, Marion County. Several of us got together in a secret place by night and formed ourselves into a military company. There were fifteen of us. By the advice of an innocent connected with the organization we called ourselves the Marion Rangers. . . .

We occupied an old maple sugar camp, whose half-rotted troughs were still propped against the trees. A long corn-crib served for sleeping quarters for the battalion. On our left, half a mile away, were Mason's farm and house; and he was a friend to the cause. Shortly after noon the farmers began to arrive from several directions, with

147

mules and horses for our use, and these they lent us for as long as the war might last, which they judged would be about three months. The animals were of all sizes, all colors, and all breeds. They were mainly young and frisky, and nobody in the command could stay on them long at a time; for we were town boys, and ignorant of horsemanship. . . .

For a time life was idly delicious, it was perfect; there was nothing to mar it. Then came some farmers with an alarm one day. They said it was rumored that the enemy were advancing in our direction from over Hyde's prairie. The result was a sharp stir among us, and general consternation. It was a rude awakening from our pleasant trance. The rumor was but a rumor—nothing definite about it; so, in the confusion, we did not know which way to retreat. Lyman was for not retreating at all in these uncertain circumstances; but he found that if he tried to maintain that attitude he would fare badly, for the command were in no humor to put up with insubordination. So he yielded the point and called a council of war—to consist of himself and the three other officers; but the privates made such a fuss about being left out that we had to allow them to remain, for they were already present, and doing the most of the talking too. The question was, which way to retreat; but all were so flurried that nobody seemed to have even a guess to offer. Except Lyman. He explained in a few calm words that, inasmuch as the enemy were approaching from over Hyde's prairie, our course was simple: all we had to do was not to retreat *towards* him; any other direction would answer our needs perfectly. Everybody saw in a moment how true this was, and how wise; so Lyman got a great many compliments. It was now decided

148

that we should fall back on Mason's farm.

It was after dark by this time, and as we could not know how soon the enemy might arrive, it did not seem best to try to take the horses and things with us; so we only took the guns and ammunition, and started at once. The route was very rough and hilly and rocky, and presently the night grew very black and rain began to fall; so we had a troublesome time of it, struggling and stumbling along in the dark; and soon some person slipped and fell, and then the next person behind stumbled over him and fell, and so did the rest, one after the other; and then Bowers came with the keg of powder in his arms, while the command were all mixed together, arms and legs, on the muddy slope; and so he fell, of course, with the keg, and this started the whole detachment down the hill in a body, and they landed in the brook at the bottom in a pile, and each that was undermost pulling the hair and scratching and biting those that were on top of him; and those that were being scratched and bitten scratching and biting the rest in their turn, and all saying they would die before they would ever go to war again if they ever got out of this brook this time, and the invader might rot for all they cared, and the country along with him—and all such talk as that, which was dismal to hear and take part in, in such smothered, low voices, and such a grisly dark place and so wet, and the enemy, maybe, coming any moment. . . .

We resolved to stay still and be comfortable. It was a fine warlike resolution, and no doubt we all felt the stir of it in our veins—for a moment. We had been having a very jolly time, that was full of horse-play and school-boy hilarity; but that cooled down now, and presently the fast-

149

waning fire of forced jokes and forced laughs died out altogether, and the company became silent. Silent and nervous. And soon uneasy—worried—apprehensive. We had said we would stay, and we were committed. We could have been persuaded to go, but there was nobody brave enough to suggest it. An almost noiseless movement presently began in the dark by a general but unvoiced impulse. When the movement was completed each man knew that he was not the only person who had crept to the front wall and had his eye at a crack between the logs. No, we were all there; all there with our hearts in our throats, and staring out towards the sugar-troughs where the forest footpath came through. It was late, and there was a deep woodsy stillness everywhere. There was a veiled moonlight, which was only just strong enough to enable us to mark the general shape of objects. Presently a muffled sound caught our ears, and we recognized it as the hoof-beats of a horse or horses. And right away a figure appeared in the forest path; it could have been made of smoke, its mass had so little sharpness of outline. It was a man on horseback, and it seemed to me that there were others behind him. I got hold of a gun in the dark, and pushed it through a crack between the logs, hardly knowing what I was doing, I was so dazed with fright. Somebody said "Fire!" I pulled the trigger. I seemed to see a hundred flashes and hear a hundred reports; then I saw the man fall down out of the saddle. My first feeling was of surprised gratification; my first impulse was an apprentice sportsman's impulse to run and pick up his game. Somebody said, hardly audibly, "Good—we've got him!—wait for the rest." But the rest did not come. We waited—listened—still no more came. There was not a sound, not

150

the whisper of a leaf; just perfect stillness; an uncanny kind of stillness, which was all the more uncanny on account of the damp, earthy, late-night smells now rising and pervading it. Then, wondering, we crept stealthily out, and approached the man. When we got to him the moon revealed him distinctly. He was lying on his back, with his arms abroad; his mouth was open and his chest heaving with long gasps, and his white shirt-front was all splashed with blood. The thought shot through me that I was a murderer; that I had killed a man—a man who had never done me any harm. That was the coldest sensation that ever went through my marrow. I was down by him in a moment, helplessly stroking his forehead; and I would have given anything then—my own life freely—to make him again what he had been five minutes before. And all the boys seemed to be feeling in the same way; they hung over him, full of pitying interest, and tried all they could to help him, and said all sorts of regretful things. They had forgotten all about the enemy; they thought only of this one forlorn unit of the foe. Once my imagination persuaded me that the dying man gave me a reproachful look out of his shadowy eyes, and it seemed to me that I could rather he had stabbed me than done that. He muttered and mumbled like a dreamer in his sleep about his wife and his child; and I thought with a new despair, "This thing that I have done does not end with him; it falls upon *them* too, and they never did me any harm, any more than he."

In a little while the man was dead. He was killed in war; killed in fair and legitimate war; killed in battle, as you may say; and yet he was as sincerely mourned by the opposing force as if he had been their brother. The boys stood there a half-hour sorrowing over him, and recalling the details of the tragedy, and wondering who he might be, and if he were a spy, and saying that if it were to do over again they would not hurt him unless he attacked them first. It soon came out that mine was not the only shot fired; there were five others—a division of the guilt which was a great relief to me, since it in some degree lightened and diminished the burden I was carrying. There were six shots fired at once; but I was not in my right mind at the time, and my heated imagination had magnified my one shot into a volley.

The man was not in uniform, and was not armed. He was a stranger in the country; that was all we ever found out about him. The thought of him got to preying upon me every night; I could not get rid of it. I could not drive it away, the taking of that unoffending life seemed such a wanton thing. And it seemed an epitome of war; that all war must be just that—the killing of strangers against whom you feel no personal animosity; strangers whom, in other circumstances, you would help if you found them in trouble, and who would help you if you needed it. My campaign was spoiled. It seemed to me that I was not rightly equipped for this awful business; that war was intended for men, and I for a child's nurse. I resolved to retire from this avocation of sham soldiership while I could save some remnant of my self-respect. . . .

From "The Private History of a Campaign That Failed,"
Mark Twain, in *Century Magazine*, December 1885.

Twain explained that he had "resigned" from military service after two weeks because he was "incapacitated by fatigue through persistent retreating." His devotion to the

152

Southern cause evaporated quickly, and he moved west to Nevada with his brother Orion. With Twain missing, the Union was ultimately able to hold on to Missouri.

That part of the West witnessed the terrors of guerrilla warfare as irregular bands of Confederate sympathizers roved the border country of Missouri and Kansas. One of the most appalling episodes occurred at Lawrence, Kansas, when a band of nearly five hundred men led by William Quantrill ravaged the town, burned it to the ground, and murdered one hundred and fifty men, women, and children. Gurdon Grovenor, one of the few people who escaped, gives this report of what he saw:

THE RAID OCCURRED on the morning of Aug. 21st, 1863. It was a clear, warm, still morning, in the midst of one of the hot, dry, dusty spells of weather common in Kansas in the month of August. The guerrillas reached Lawrence just before sunrise after an all night's ride from the border of Missouri. Myself and family were yet in bed and asleep. They passed directly by our house, and we were awakened by their yelling and shouting. . . .

They first made for the main street, passing up as far as the Eldridge House to see if they were going to meet with any opposition, and when they found none they scattered out all over town, killing, stealing and burning. We hastily dressed ourselves and closed up the house tightly as possible and began to talk over what was best to do. My first thought was to get away to some hiding place, but on looking out there seemed no possibility of that as the enemy were everywhere, and I had a feeling that I ought not to leave my family, a young wife and two children, one a babe of three months old, and so we sat down and

153

Quantrill's devastating raid on Lawrence, Kansas, as sketched by a Union cavalryman.

awaited developments. We saw men shot down and fires shooting up in all directions.

Just on the north of our house, a half a block away and in full view, was a camp of recruits twenty-two in all, not yet mustered into service and unarmed. They were awakened by the noise, got up and started to run but were all shot down but five. I saw this wholesale shooting from my window, and it was a sight to strike terror to a stouter heart than mine. But we had not long to wait before our time came. Three of the guerrillas came to the house, stepped up on the front porch, and with the butt of a musket smashed in one of the front windows; my wife opened the door and let them in. They ransacked the house, talked and swore and threatened a good deal, but offered no violence. They set the house on fire above and

154

below, took such things as they fancied, and left. After they had gone I put the fire out below, but above it had got too strong a hold, and I could not put it out.

Not long after a single man rode up to the front gate; he was a villainous looking fellow, and was doubly villainous from too much whiskey. He saw me standing back in the hall of the house, and with a terrible oath he ordered me to come out. I stepped out on the piazza, and he leveled his pistol at me and said, "Are you union or secesh?"

It was my time of trial; my wife with her little one in her arms, and our little boy clinging to her side, was standing just a little ways from me. My life seemingly hung on my answer, my position may be imagined but it cannot be described. The thought ran through me like an electric shock, that I could not say that I was a secessionist, and deny my loyalty to my country; that I would rather die than to live and face that disgrace; and so I answered that I was a union man. He snapped his pistol but it failed to fire. I stepped back into the house and he rode around to the north door and met me there, and snapped his pistol at me again, and this time it failed. Was there a providence in this?

Just then a party of a half dozen of the raiders came riding towards the house from the north, and seeing my enemy, hallooed to him "Don't shoot that man." They rode up to the gate and told me to come there; I did so and my would be murderer came up to me and placed the muzzle of his revolver in my ear. It was not a pleasant place to be in, but the leader of the new crowd told him not to shoot, but to let me alone until he could inquire about me, so he asked me if I had ever been down in Missouri stealing niggers or horses; I told him "No that

I never had been in Missouri, except to cross the state going and coming from the east." This seemed to be satisfactory so he told my old enemy to let me alone and not to kill me. This seemed to make him very angry, and he cursed me terribly, but I ventured to put my hand up and push away his revolver. The leader of the party then told me if I did not expect to get killed, I must get out of sight, that they were all getting drunk, and would kill everybody they saw; I told him that that was what I had wanted to do all the morning, but I could not; "Well," he says, "you must hide or get killed." And they all rode away.

After they had gone I told my wife that I would go into the cellar, and stay until the fire reached me, and if any more of the raiders inquired for me to tell them that I had been taken a prisoner and carried off. . . .

The cellar of my house was under the ell and the fire was in the front and in the upper story. There was an outside bulk-head door, where I knew I could get out after the fire had reached the floor above me. I had not been in the cellar long before my wife came and said they had just killed my neighbor across the street.

Soon after the notorious Bill Anderson, passing by the house, saw my wife standing in the yard, stopped and commenced talking with her; told her how many men he had killed that morning, and inquiring where her husband was; she told him that he had been taken prisoner and carried away—was it my wife's duty to tell him the truth, tell him where I was and let him come and shoot me as he would a dog, which he would have done? Awhile after my wife came and said she thought the raiders had all gone, and so I came out of my prison just as the fire was eating through the floor over my head, thankful that I had passed through that dreadful ordeal and was safe.

Such was my experience during those four or five terrible hours. Our home and its contents was in ashes, but so thankful were we that my life was spared that we thought but little of our pecuniary loss. After the raiders had left and the people could get out on the street, a most desolate and sickening sight met their view. The whole business part of the town, except two stores, was in ashes. The bodies of dead men, some of them partly burned away, were laying in all directions. A large number of dwellings were burned to the ground, and the moaning of the grief stricken people was heard from all sides. . . .

From the report of Gurdon Grovenor, in *Quantrill and the Border Wars*, William E. Connelly, Torch Press, 1910.

UNDER SIEGE

The most wearing time in war for soldiers—and civilians— is the siege. A siege may last for weeks, months, or even years. It is the time when an army is positioned in front of a fortified place in order to force its surrender. The besiegers simply wait for the army penned up inside to give up because supplies and morale are low, or they may hasten surrender by bombardment and a series of assaults.

Both armies in the Civil War laid siege to enemy positions—the Union troops to at least a dozen major fortresses and many minor ones, and the Confederates to only a few large towns. Interestingly, Union forces never quit a siege once they began it. They finally captured every place they meant to. Nor did they ever surrender a position of their own under siege. The Rebels, however, never captured a position they besieged, and they were always forced to give up any fortress they tried to hold.

The siege of Vicksburg, a city high on a bluff above the Mississippi River, was a prime target of the Union campaign for the river. General Grant hoped to cut off the West from the other Rebel states, and to open up passage from the Gulf of Mexico to the North. By the spring of 1862 much of this had been achieved, except for taking Vicksburg and Port Hudson.

Grant made two attacks upon Vicksburg, but was repulsed. Then he decided to lay siege to the city, with an army of seventy thousand and over two hundred guns. After a six-week bombardment, on July 4, 1863, General Pemberton surrendered the city and over thirty thousand troops, the largest haul of manpower up to that time.

A Union woman (we don't know her name), caught somehow inside Vicksburg amid the Southerners, describes the tension and danger in a diary she kept:

MARCH 20, 1863—The slow shelling of Vicksburg goes on all the time, and we have grown indifferent. It does not at present interrupt or interfere with daily avocations, but I suspect they are only getting the range of different points; and when they have them all complete, showers of shot

158

During the siege of Vicksburg Federal soldiers put up log breast-works, pitched tents, and cooked under the thunder of the guns.

will rain on us all at once. Noncombatants have been ordered to leave or prepare accordingly. Those who are to stay are having caves built. Cave-digging has become a regular business; prices range from twenty to fifty dollars, according to size of cave. Two diggers worked at ours a week and charged thirty dollars. It is well made in the hill that slopes just in the rear of the house, and well propped with thick posts, as they all are. It has a shelf also, for holding a light or water. When we went in this evening and sat down, the earthy, suffocating feeling, as of a living tomb, was dreadful to me. I fear I shall risk death outside rather than melt in that dark furnace. The hills are so honeycombed with caves that the streets look like avenues in a cemetery. . . .

APRIL 28—I never understood before the full force of those questions—what shall we eat? what shall we drink?

and wherewithal shall we be clothed? We have no prophet of the Lord at whose prayer the meal and oil will not waste. Such minute attention must be given the wardrobe to preserve it that I have learned to darn like an artist. Making shoes is now another accomplishment. Mine were in tatters. H. came across a moth-eaten pair that he bought me, giving ten dollars, I think, and they fell into rags when I tried to wear them; but the soles were good, and that has helped me to shoes. A pair of old coat sleeves saved— nothing is thrown away now—was in my trunk. I cut an exact pattern from my old shoes, laid it on the sleeves, and cut out thus good uppers and sewed them carefully; then soaked the soles and sewed the cloth to them. I am so proud of these homemade shoes, think I'll put them in a glass case when the war is over, as an heirloom. . . .

I have but a dozen pins remaining, so many I gave away. Every time these are used they are straightened and kept from rust. All these curious labors are performed while the shells are leisurely screaming through the air; but as long as we are out of range we don't worry. For many nights we have had but little sleep, because the Federal gunboats have been running past the batteries. The uproar when this is happening is phenomenal. The first night the thundering artillery burst the bars of sleep, we thought it an attack by the river. To get into garments and rush upstairs was the work of a moment. From the upper gallery we have a fine view of the river, and soon a red glare lit up the scene and showed a small boat, towing two large barges, gliding by. The Confederates had set fire to a house near the bank. Another night, eight boats ran by, throwing a shower of shot, and two burning houses made the river clear as day. One of the batteries has a remarkable gun they call "Whistling Dick," because of the screeching, whistling sound it gives, and certainly it does sound like a tortured thing. Added to all this is the indescribable Confederate yell, which is a soul-harrowing sound to hear. . . . Yesterday the *Cincinnati* attempted to go by in daylight, but was disabled and sunk. It was a pitiful sight; we could not see the finale, though we saw her rendered helpless. . . .

MAY 28—The regular siege has continued. We are utterly cut off from the world, surrounded by a circle of fire. Would it be wise like the scorpion to sting ourselves to death? The fiery shower of shells goes on day and night. H.'s occupation, of course, is gone; his office closed. Every man has to carry a pass in his pocket. People do nothing but eat what they can get, sleep when they can, and dodge the shells. There are three intervals when the shelling stops, either for the guns to cool or for the gunners' meals, I suppose—about eight in the morning, the same in the evening, and at noon. In that time we have both to prepare and eat ours. Clothing cannot be washed or anything else done. On the 19th and 22d, when the assaults were made on the lines, I watched the soldiers cooking on the green opposite. The half-spent balls coming all the way from those lines were flying so thick that they were obliged to dodge at every turn. At all the caves I could see from my high perch, people were sitting, eating their poor suppers at the cave doors, ready to plunge in again. As the first shell again flew they dived, and not a human being was visible. The sharp crackle of the musketry firing was a strong contrast to the scream of the bombs. I think all the dogs and cats must be killed or starved; we don't see any more pitiful animals prowling around. . . .

JUNE 25—A horrible day. The most horrible yet to me, because I've lost my nerve. We were all in the cellar, when a shell came tearing through the roof, burst upstairs, tore up that room, and the pieces coming through both floors down into the cellar, one of them tore open the leg of H.'s pantaloons. This was tangible proof the cellar was no place of protection from them. On the heels of this came Mr. J. to tell us that young Mrs. P. had had her thighbone crushed. When Martha went for the milk she came back horror-stricken to tell us the black girl there had her arm taken off by a shell. For the first time I quailed. I do not think people who are physically brave deserve much credit for it; it is a matter of nerves. In this way I am constitutionally brave, and seldom think of danger till it is over; and death has not the terrors for me it has for some others. Every night I had lain down expecting death, and every morning rose to the same prospect, without being unnerved. It was for H. I trembled. But now I first seemed to realize that something worse than death might come: I might be crippled, and not killed. Life, without all one's powers and limbs, was a thought that broke down my courage. I said to H., "You must get me out of this horrible place; I cannot stay; I know I shall be crippled." Now the regret comes that I lost control, because H. is worried, and has lost his composure, because my coolness has broken down. . . .

From "A Woman's Diary of the Siege of Vicksburg," George W. Cable, ed., *Century Magazine*, VIII, 1885.

Blacks freed by advancing Union troops not only joined the armed forces but did a great variety of labor service. Here they dig a canal for General Grant during the siege of Vicksburg.

With the capture of Vicksburg and Port Hudson the Union won control of the central Mississippi Valley. The fighting moved into Tennessee, toward Chattanooga. That city was the gateway to the East. The Federals needed to take it in order to advance into Georgia. The armies met at Chickamauga, and the Federals, ironically, were forced

163

*to retire into Chattanooga, the city they had hoped to cap-
ture. But now they were besieged in it. Union troops from
other armies were sent toward the city to relieve it, and in
November, at the battle of Lookout Mountain and Missionary Ridge, they succeeded in routing the Confederates. So
the siege was broken; the Union had split the Confederacy
vertically.*

*W. F. G. Shanks, a war correspondent with the Union
troops inside Chattanooga, gives us these notes on the siege:*

IF THERE WAS little of beauty or elegance in the place
when our troops retreated into it from Chickamauga,
there was a great deal less a fortnight subsequently. Like
many another Southern town Chattanooga grew suddenly
old; one might say it turned gray during the brief but dark
night of the siege. . . . Residences were turned into block-
houses; black bastions sprang up in former vineyards; rifle
pits were run through the graveyards; and soon a long line
of works stretched from the river above to the river below
the city, bending crescentlike around it, as if it were a huge
bow of iron, and rendering it impregnable. For a fortnight
the whole army worked on the fortifications, and it became literally a walled city. . . .

The winter quarters of the troops, composed of small
dog-kennel-shaped huts, built of boards and roofed over
with the shelter-tents with which the soldiers were provided, were scattered all over the town in valley and on
hillside. . . .

The camps of the soldiers were not cantonments in the
proper sense of the term. The immediate presence and
threatening proximity of the enemy rendered it necessary
to safety and discipline that the troops should encamp in

164

the regular order of regiments and brigades, so as to be prepared to form at the sound of alarm, ready to repulse or to make an attack. Instead, therefore, of camping indiscriminately in houses as they stood, the men tore down the houses and fences, and of the framework built their huts, and of the bricks their chimneys and fireplaces. . . .

Life in Chattanooga during the two months of the siege was dreary enough. There was no fighting to do; the enemy daily threw a few shells from the top of Lookout Mountain into our camps, but they were too wise to attack with infantry the works which soon encircled the city. Bragg preferred to rely for the final reduction of the garrison upon his ally famine, a very formidable antagonist did our men find him in the end. Famine became a familiar friend. . . . The men were put on quarter rations. . . . Men cannot dig fortifications and fight very long on such rations; and the whole army was half famished. I have often seen hundreds of soldiers following behind the wagon trains which had just arrived, picking out of the mud the crumbs of bread, coffee, rice, etc., which were wasted from the boxes and sacks by the rattling of the wagons over the stones. Nothing was wasted in those days, and though the inspectors would frequently condemn whole wagon loads of provisions as spoiled by exposure during the trip, and order the contents to be thrown away, the soldiers or citizens always found some use for it. . . .

From "Chattanooga, and How We Held It,"
W. F. G. Shanks, *Harper's New Monthly Magazine*, XXXVI, 1867–68.

On the Virginia front, the Union gathered its forces to capture the Confederate capital at Richmond. In March

1864 Lincoln made General Grant supreme commander of the Union armies. Grant's aim was to hammer relentlessly at Lee's army until he had destroyed enough of it to force surrender. Lee resisted with great skill, and the battles in the Wilderness in May and Cold Harbor in June cost Grant nearly sixty thousand casualties, and Lee half as much. But Lee was far less able to take such heavy punishment.

In mid-June Grant moved his forces to a base at the James River, to attack from the south. It worked, and he pinned Lee's army twenty miles below Richmond. Thus he approached the capital from the rear, while cutting off its transportation links with the South. But when he failed to take Petersburg by assault, he dug in to besiege it for what would be nine months, the longest siege of the war. An attempt to tunnel under the town and explode a huge mine (the "Crater" referred to in the passage that follows) cost the Union many men, but failed to break the siege. Not until April 1865 did Petersburg surrender.

A Confederate soldier, Luther R. Mills of North Carolina, penned inside Petersburg, writes his brother John about the breakdown of rebel morale shortly before surrender:

SOMETHING IS about to happen. I know not what. Nearly everyone who will express an opinion says Gen'l Lee is about to evacuate Petersburg. . . . I go down the lines, I see the marks of shot and shell, I see where fell my comrades, the Crater, the grave of fifteen hundred Yankees, when I go to the rear I see little mounds of dirt, some with headboards, some with none, some with shoes protruding, some with a small pile of bones on one side near the end showing where a hand was left uncovered, in fact every-

166

thing near shows desperate fighting. And here I would rather "fight it out." If Petersburg and Richmond is evacuated—from what I have seen and heard in the army—our cause will be hopeless. It is useless to conceal the truth any longer. Many of our people at home have become so demoralized that they write to their husbands, sons and brothers that desertion now is not dishonorable. It would be impossible to keep the army from straggling to a ruinous extent if we evacuate. I have just received an order from Wise to carry out on picket tonight a rifle and ten rounds of cartridges to shoot men when they desert. The men seem to think desertion no crime and hence never shoot a deserter when he goes over—they always shoot but never hit. . . .

From "Letters of Luther Rice Mills—A Confederate Soldier," George D. Harmon, ed., *North Carolina Historical Review,* IV, July 1927.

∼27∼

MARCHING THROUGH GEORGIA

*As Grant and Lee stood opposite each other at Petersburg,
Union armies were chopping up the Confederacy from the
rear. Vicksburg had already been cut away, then Chickamauga and Chattanooga. And now General William
Tecumseh Sherman was on his march through Georgia
with one hundred thousand men. All along the way Sherman was harried by Confederate defensive actions under
General Joseph E. Johnston. A battle at New Hope Church
in May cost the Yankees much, as Captain Samuel T.
Foster of the Confederate Texas Brigade observes:*

MAY 28TH, 1864—About sun-up this morning we were
relieved and ordered back to the Brigade—and we have to
pass over the dead Yanks of the battlefield of yesterday;
and here I beheld that which I cannot describe; and which
I hope never see again, dead men meet the eye in every
direction, and in one place I stopped and counted 50 dead
men in a circle of 30 ft. of me. Men lying in all sorts of
shapes and [illegible] just as they had fallen, and it seems
like they have nearly all been shot in the head, and a great
number of them have their skulls bursted open and their
brains running out, quite a number that way. I have seen
many dead men, and seen them wounded and crippled in
various ways, have seen their limbs cut off, but I never saw
anything before that made me sick, like looking at the

168

During the summer that Sherman's troops fought in Georgia, Sheridan's troops forage for supplies as they march through the Shenandoah Valley, killing livestock and burning granaries and buildings.

brains of these men did. I do believe that if a soldier could be made to faint, that I would have fainted if I had not passed on and got out of that place as soon as I did—We learn thru Col. Wilkes that we killed 703 dead on the ground, and captured near 350 prisoners. . . .

Late in July Sherman's troops were only eight miles from Atlanta. The Confederates, impatient with Johnston's delaying tactics, had replaced him with General John B. Hood. He attacked Sherman in pitched battle but suffered heavy losses. Captain Foster was in the midst of that bloody tangle:

169

JULY 21—Made breastworks of logs, and by nine o'clock A.M. the Yanks artillery open on us from our left, their shell enfilading our lines. They have heard us chopping down trees and building our works and have our range— and the woods are so thick we can't see them. Their artillery are killing our men very fast—One company just to my left after finishing their works sat down to rest in a little ditch they had dug, when a shell came and took them at one end and killed and crippled every man in the ditch. Knocked one man in a hundred pieces—one hand and arm went over the works and his cartridge box was ten feet up in a tree.

My company had completed their works when as I was lying down resting on my elbow—and another man in about the same position with our heads about two feet apart and our feet in opposite directions, a shell exploded just between us—blowing me one way and him the other, hurting neither one of us but killing three men about 10 ft. from us eating their breakfast.

About the middle of the day the small arms open on us in front of us and as soon as our pickets came in a general fire opens along our line. . . .

Here is where Lt. Boerner of Capt. Flys Co. and Bud Martin same company were killed—both shot in the head, and while we were driving the Yanks out from our rear, one man (Joe Harrison) of my Company ran up to a Yank, that was cursing a wounded Confed, put the muzzle of his gun to his back and blew him up. . . .

When the roar of battle ended, Captain Foster made another entry in his diary:

As Sherman's troops moved into the deep South, they destroyed communications useful to the enemy, including this railroad bridge over the Ogeechee River.

JULY 23—All quiet this morning, after a terrible day yesterday all along the lines.

Our men are getting boots, hats, etc., watches, knives, etc. off of the dead Yanks near us in the woods—lots of them.

Alf Neil and Ogle Love come back this morning, having been overheated yesterday, and retired. Our dead have all been buried, and the Yanks will be as soon as they can do so.

We cook and eat, talk and laugh with the enemy's dead lying all about us as though they were so many logs.

From *One of Cleburne's Command: The Civil War Reminiscences and Diary of Captain Samuel T. Foster, Texas Brigade, CSA*, Norman D. Brown, ed., University of Texas Press, 1980.

171

*Atlanta fell to Sherman on September 2. The news stiff-
ened Northern morale and helped Lincoln win victory in his
campaign for reelection to the presidency that fall. In mid-
November Sherman set out with sixty thousand troops on
his march to the sea. Sweeping across Georgia, his men
systematically destroyed everything in their path useful to
the Confederates—railroads, factories, cotton gins, warehouses, bridges, public buildings.*

*The Union soldiers were told to live off the country. The
foragers, called Sherman's "Bummers," are described by
Lieutenant Charles Booth of the Third Division:*

I MUST TELL you a little about a class in our army . . .
called "Bummers." Imagine a fellow with a gun and accoutrements, with a plug hat, a captured militia plume in
it, a citizen's saddle, with a bed quilt or tablecloth, upon
an animal whose ears are the larger part of the whole. Let
us take an inventory of his stock as he rides into camp at
night. Poor fellow! He has rode upon that knock-kneed,
shaved-tail, rail-fence mule over 30 miles, has fought the
brush and mud, and passed through untold dangers, and
all for his load, which consists of, first, a bundle of fodder
for his mule; second, three hams, a sack of meal, a peck
of potatoes; third, a fresh bed quilt, the old mother's coffee
pot, a jug of vinegar and a bed cord. You call him an old,
steady bummer. I'll give you one more picture. Here
comes a squad of eighteen or nineteen, no two alike. Look
at the chickens, geese, beehives; see that little fellow with
a huge hog strapped upon his nag's back. There rides the
commander, a lieutenant, completely happy, for the day
has been a good one, and his detail has got enough for a
day's good supply for his regiment.

172

These "Bummers" were detailed for foragers, and upon them the army depended for subsistence; for be it known that we started with a very small stock of supplies, and our campaign was lengthened after starting from our base (Savannah), consequently the "Bummers" were the life of the army. About 5,000 strong, not a field or house or barn but was searched by them; not a town or hamlet but the "infernal bummers" managed to plunder. They met the enemy at Fayetteville, and drove him across Cape Fear river; they entered Columbia as skirmishers, not only for "Johnnies," but for meat and bread and goodies.

Many outrages were committed by them. To enter a house and find the feather bed ripped open, the wardrobes ransacked, chests stripped of contents, looking glasses taken from the walls, cooking utensils gone, and all the corn meal and bacon missing, bed quilts stripped from the beds, the last jar of pickles gone, was no uncommon sight, and one to make a soldier blush with indignation. Every effort that could be made was made to check the demoralization of the foragers; but the occupation tended to demoralization, and "the army must be fed, and the Bummers must feed us." Thus we reasoned, but deprecated the means used to bring about the result. Some would discriminate, others would not, and thus the few have caused a great deal of unnecessary suffering. . . .

From a letter written by Charles A. Booth and dated March 27, 1865, in *The Star Corps*, G. S. Bradley, 1865.

How the Georgians felt as Sherman's destroyers marched through is told in a diary written by Eliza Andrews:

DECEMBER 24, 1864—About three miles from Sparta we struck the "burnt country," as it is well named by the natives, and then I could better understand the wrath and desperation of these poor people. I almost felt as if I should like to hang a Yankee myself. There was hardly a fence left standing all the way from Sparta to Gordon. The fields were trampled down and the road was lined with carcasses of horses, hogs, and cattle that the invaders, unable either to consume or to carry away with them, had wantonly shot down, to starve out the people and prevent them from making their crops. The stench in some places was unbearable; every few hundred yards we had to hold our noses or stop them with the cologne Mrs. Elzey had given us, and it proved a great boon. The dwellings that were standing all showed signs of pillage, and on every plantation we saw the charred remains of the ginhouse and packing screw, while here and there lone chimney stacks, "Sherman's sentinels," told of homes laid in ashes. The infamous wretches! I couldn't wonder now that these poor people should want to put a rope round the neck of every red-handed "devil of them" they could lay their hands on. Hayricks and fodder stacks were demolished, corncribs were empty, and every bale of cotton that could be found was burnt by the savages. I saw no grain of any sort except little patches they had spilled when feeding their horses and which there was not even a chicken left in the country to eat. A bag of oats might have lain any-where along the road without danger from the beasts of the field, though I cannot say it would have been safe from the assaults of hungry man.

Crowds of soldiers were tramping over the road in both directions; it was like traveling through the streets of a populous town all day. They were mostly on foot, and I saw numbers seated on the roadside greedily eating raw turnips, meat skins, parched corn—anything they could find, even picking up the loose grains that Sherman's horses had left. . . .

From *The War-Time Journal of a Georgia Girl*,
Eliza Frances Andrews, Appleton, 1908.

Sherman's troops swept northward from Georgia, tearing up the Carolinas, burning towns as they went. Part of South Carolina's capital, Columbia, was set afire, though no one agrees how. With Sherman's army was George W. Pepper, who describes the horror of the burning city:

IN THE EVENING of the 17th of February, before our troops entered the town, several bales of cotton were set on fire, it was supposed, by some rebel citizen. The wind blowing very heavily at the time, it spread with great rapidity, and in a few hours a whole block of large buildings, in Richardson Street, was in flames. From these it caught to the extensive rebel storerooms, to the Episcopal Church, then to the Ursuline Convent, and thence to nearly every street in the city. Vast quantities of corn, flour, sugar, etc., were destroyed. The passenger depots, used as storehouses, and filled with blankets and various other articles, were burned. Had it not been for the activity and magnanimous conduct of our troops, there would not be one house as a shelter for those who fled from the smoking ruins of their burning dwellings.

I shall never forget the terrible scenes of that night. The sight was heartrending; men, women and children rushed into the streets from the showers of ashes and burning brands that were falling in all directions. The houses were soon emptied. Half-eaten suppers remained on splendid tables. The infuriated Negroes dashed four abreast through the deserted mansions, soon to be in flames. They glut their eyes on trunks and wardrobes. A few drunken soldiers push their bayonets into beds and tapestry. The cushioned carpets and splendidly gilt books are scattered everywhere. The mob spares nothing; ticks are ripped open, and rich laces lie in tatters. Chandeliers and crimson hangings are utterly destroyed. Silk dresses, just imported, costing ten thousand dollars, in long strips, stream out of the windows, and the Negroes below catch them, and make apron strings of them.

Down into cellars and vaults the sable mob rushes, and brings up mouldy-topped bottles of wine. Sitting on the fragments of pianos they drink confusion to their runaway masters. The scene beggars all description. Timid and frantic women, in all the corners of the streets—they have flung themselves from their burning dwellings, and with their frightened little ones are gazing at the smouldering remains of their former elegant homes. The storm increases. At eleven o'clock it begins to blow from the southwest, and the fire spreads over the city in the opposite direction.

The next morning, at two o'clock, every street was burning, and the whole city was awfully and solemnly illuminated. The turnout on the streets is immense, and the utmost excitement prevailed. Thousands of soldiers did their best endeavors to stop the terrible display of fire. In vain! The streets through which the fire raged were the principal ones of the place. Old men pronounced it the most terrible scene they had ever beheld. Think of twenty thousand, including all classes, suddenly turned out of doors. Scores who rose that morning with their thousands are now penniless, homeless! Refined and cultivated ladies are seen, in beseeching attitudes, calling for help. They convulsively clasp their little ones to their bosoms, and then utter a piercing prayer to Heaven for deliverance. Few who were present were unmoved at these scenes, and tears could be seen on many a soldier's cheek.

Hark! What a tremendous crash! The very earth quakes. It is the explosion of a vast quantity of powder in the arsenal. What a gigantic fire—it blazes on all the adjacent squares! Thousands gather around it. The engines are dashing hither and thither.

The grand conflagration which destroyed the city commenced about dark. The fire started near the rear of the jail. A high wind prevailed, and in a short time the flames were in full and unconquerable progress. The sky was one broad sheet of flame, above which, amid the lurid smoke, drifted in eddying circles a myriad of sparks. These falling, scattered the seeds of conflagration on every side. The monotone of the hissing, waving, leaping tongues of flame, as they careered on their wild course, alone filled hearts with dismay. The air was like that of a furnace. The arsenal was burned to the ground. This vast and magnificent building was wrapt in flame and smoke. As the wind swept the dense volumes away to the northeast, the southern slope of the roof appeared composed of molten gold, instinct with life and motion. It soon fell with a tremendous crash, and immediately, as if with fiendish joy, the destructive element in a high column of mingled fire and smoke leaped unto the very skies. Morning revealed to some extent the broad sweep of destruction. Eighty-five blocks in the city were burned, and Columbia is the Palmyra in the desert. Five thousand citizens were houseless. From the State House to Cottontown, nothing but blackened ruins remained. The beautiful city of Columbia no longer existed. It is a mass of charred ruins—Herculaneum buried in ashes. . . .

South Carolina is reaping at last the consequence of her treason. . . .

From *Personal Recollections of Sherman's Campaigns in Georgia and the Carolinas*, George W. Pepper, 1866.

∽ 28 ∼

SURRENDER—AND
ASSASSINATION

As the winter months of early 1865 came on, the Confederacy fell apart. Union armies occupied many important sections of the South, and the devastation of crops spread hunger everywhere. Riots and demonstrations against the Confederate government broke out in Southern cities. Rebel army morale crumbled, and mass desertions left the army with only a third of its manpower. In desperation the

178

Confederate Congress authorized arming the slaves, but it was an empty gesture.

On March 4 President Lincoln again took the oath of office and gave his second inaugural address. He appealed to the people not to seek vengeance: "With malice toward none; with charity for all . . . let us strive on to finish the work we are in; to bind up the nation's wounds—to do all which may achieve and cherish a just and lasting peace."

On April 2 Lee evacuated Petersburg and Richmond, with Grant pursuing him. A Union officer, R. B. Prescott of Massachusetts, took part in the capture of Richmond, and describes the scene as he entered the Confederate capital with his troops:

EVERY MOMENT THE light we had seen over Richmond on starting became more and more brilliant. Above it hung great clouds of heavy smoke, and as we drew nearer there arose a confused murmur now swelling into a loud roar and then subsiding, and again swelling into a great tumult of excited voices, while at frequent intervals short, sharp explosions were heard as of the discharge of field artillery. Weary, breathless, hungry, begrimed with dust and perspiration, but eager and excited, we pushed on, and at half-past six o'clock in the morning I stood with about two thirds of my men on the summit of a hill and looked down upon the grandest and most appalling sight that my eyes ever beheld. Richmond was literally a sea of flame, out of which the church steeples could be seen protruding here and there, while over all hung a canopy of dense black smoke, lighted up now and then by the bursting shells from the numerous arsenals scattered throughout the city. . . .

179

SURRENDER OF GEN. LEE!

"The Year of Jubilee has come! Let all the People Rejoice!"

200 GUNS WILL BE FIRED

On the Campus Martius,

AT 3 O'CLOCK TO-DAY, APRIL 10,

To Celebrate the Victories of our Armies.

Every Man, Woman and Child is hereby ordered to be on hand prepared to Sing and Rejoice. The crowd are expected to join in singing Patriotic Songs.

ALL PLACES OF BUSINESS MUST BE CLOSED AT 2 O'CLOCK.

Hurrah for Grant and his noble Army.

By Order of the People.

A broadside in Detroit greets the news of Lee's surrender.

The scene that met our eyes here almost baffles description. Pandemonium reigned supreme. Two large ironclads nearby in the river exploded with a deafening crash, the concussion sweeping numbers of people off their feet. The street we were in was one compact mass of frenzied people, and it was only with the greatest difficulty that we were able to force our way along. Had they been hostile our lives would not have been worth a moment's purchase.

But the poor colored people hailed our appearance with the most extravagant expressions of joy. They crowded into the ranks and besought permission to carry the soldiers' knapsacks and muskets. They clapped them on the

180

back, hung about their necks, and "God bless you" and "Thank God, the Yankees have come" resounded on every side. Women, emaciated, barefoot, with but one scanty skirt made from old bags, fell on their knees in the street, and with clasped hands and streaming eyes thanked God that their sufferings were ended at last. Others with little children, wretched little skeletons, clinging to their scanty skirts and crying with hunger and fright, pressed into the ranks and begged most piteously for food.

One woman, I distinctly remember, with three little pale, starved girls clinging about her, herself barefoot, bareheaded, thinly and miserably clad, seized my arm with a viselike grip, and begged for the love of God, for just a morsel for her starving children. They had tasted nothing since Sunday morning, and then only a spoonful of dry meal. I gave her the contents of my haversack, and one man in the ranks, a great, rough, swearing fellow, poured into her lap his entire three days' rations of pork and hard bread, thrust a ten-dollar greenback, all the money he possessed, into her hand, swearing like a pirate all the while as a means of relief to his overcharged feelings, their intensity being abundantly evident by the tears which coursed rapidly down his cheeks. . . .

The spacious capitol grounds afforded the only spot of refuge, and these were crowded with women and children, bearing in their arms and upon their heads their most cherished possessions. Piles of furniture lay scattered in every direction, and about them clustered the hungry and destitute family groups, clinging to each other with the energy of despair. One of the most touching sights amid these accumulated horrors was that of a little girl—a toddling infant—holding her kitten tightly under her arm, a dilapidated rag doll in one hand and grasping her mother's gown with the other, as they sought shelter from the showers of cinders under the capitol steps.

The constant explosion of ammunition in the arsenals seemed almost like a battle. Many citizens were killed by the flying fragments. Many were burned to death. In one house seventeen people perished from the flames. The sick, the aged, helpless and infirm, left to themselves in the general panic, could only pray for deliverance, which came to them when the flames had stifled their prayers in death.

Seven hundred and fifty thousand loaded shells in the arsenals, exploding from the heat, tore their way through houses, ploughed up the streets and the gardens, and spread death and destruction on every hand. The whole city jarred and vibrated with horrid sounds, while warehouses, stores, mills, bridges, depots, and dwellings went down by scores and hundreds. The streets leading to the railroad stations were filled with a frantic mob, pushing, struggling, cursing, trampling each other without mercy in their efforts to get away with what plunder they could carry. No troops of either army were in sight, only rebel stragglers, whose long familiarity with similar scenes rendered them, no doubt, the only cool-headed and indifferent spectators of these appalling sights. Over and above all the terrible roar of the conflagration, as it leaped from building to building, from street to street, filled the whole city with its scorching breath, and lent added horrors to the scene.

From "The Capture of Richmond," R. B. Prescott, in *Civil War Papers, Massachusetts Commandery*, 1900.

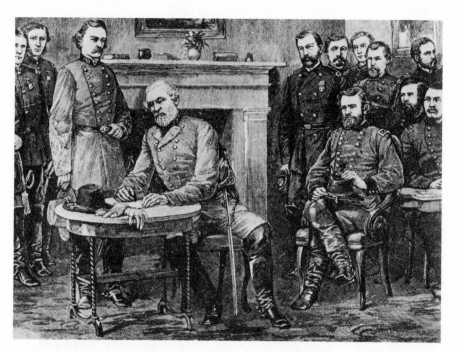

General Lee signing the terms of surrender as General Grant looks on.

Lee now had less than thirty thousand men left in his army and could go on no longer. On April 9 he met Grant at Appomattox Courthouse and accepted the generous terms of surrender. Lee's soldiers were allowed to go home, with rations supplied by the Union. Grant told his troops not to cheer because, he said, "The rebels are our countrymen again." The Confederate government simply evaporated.

On April 14 Lincoln and his wife went to see a play at Ford's Theatre in Washington. During the performance, an assassin, John Wilkes Booth, shot the president. Lincoln died the next morning without ever regaining consciousness. Gideon Welles, secretary of the navy in Lincoln's

183

cabinet, was present at the deathbed, and recorded it in his diary:

THE PRESIDENT had been carried across the street from the theater, to the house of a Mr. Peterson. We entered by ascending a flight of steps above the basement and passing through a long hall to the rear, where the President lay extended on a bed, breathing heavily. Several surgeons were present, at least six, I should think more. Among them I was glad to observe Dr. Hall, who, however, soon left. I inquired of Dr. H., as I entered, the true condition of the President. He replied the President was dead to all intents, although he might live three hours or perhaps longer.

The giant sufferer lay extended diagonally across the bed, which was not long enough for him. He had been stripped of his clothes. His large arms, which were occasionally exposed, were of a size which one would scarce have expected from his spare appearance. His slow, full respiration lifted the clothes with each breath that he took. His features were calm and striking. I had never seen them appear to better advantage than for the first hour, perhaps, that I was there. After that, his right eye began to swell and that part of his face became discolored. . . .

The room was small and overcrowded. The surgeons and members of the Cabinet were as many as should have been in the room, but there were many more, and the hall and other rooms in the front or main house were full. One of these rooms was occupied by Mrs. Lincoln and her attendants, with Miss Harris. Mr. Dixon and Mrs. Kinney came to her about twelve o'clock. About once an hour Mrs. Lincoln would repair to the bedside of her dying

184

Just four days before Lincoln was shot in Ford's Theater, this photograph was taken.

husband and with lamentation and tears remain until overcome by emotion. . . .

About 6 A.M. I experienced a feeling of faintness and for the first time after entering the room, a little past eleven, I left it and the house, and took a short walk in the open air. It was a dark and gloomy morning, and rain set in before I returned to the house, some fifteen minutes [later]. Large groups of people were gathered every few rods, all anxious and solicitous. Some one or more from each group stepped forward as I passed, to inquire into the condition of the President, and to ask if there was no hope. Intense grief was on every countenance when I replied that the President could survive but a short time. The colored people especially—and there were at this time more of them, perhaps, than of whites—were overwhelmed with grief. . . .

A little before seven, I went into the room where the dying President was rapidly drawing near the closing moments. His wife soon after made her last visit to him. The death struggle had begun. Robert, his son, stood with several others at the head of the bed. He bore himself well, but on two occasions gave way to overpowering grief and sobbed aloud, turning his head and leaning on the shoulder of Senator Sumner. The respiration of the President became suspended at intervals, and at last entirely ceased at twenty-two minutes past seven. . . .

I went after breakfast to the Executive Mansion. There was a cheerless cold rain and everything seemed gloomy. On the Avenue in front of the White House were several hundred colored people, mostly women and children, weeping and wailing their loss. This crowd did not appear to diminish through the whole of that cold, wet day; they

186

seemed not to know what was to be their fate since their great benefactor was dead, and their hopeless grief affected me more than almost anything else, though strong and brave men wept when I met them. . . .

From *Diary of Gideon Welles,* Houghton Mifflin, 1911.

～29～

PEACE, AND AFTER

If the cost of war is measured by the proportion of casualties to those who fought, the Civil War took the greatest toll of all American wars. Between thirty-three and forty percent of the combined Union and Confederate forces were casualties. The Union dead numbered some 360,000, the wounded 275,000. For the Confederates it was 258,000 dead and 100,000 wounded.

To those waiting at home for their men, reunion was bittersweet. When the Union soldier Samuel Cormany made his way back to Chambersburg, Pennsylvania, months after the war ended, his wife, Rachel, made this entry in her diary:

AUGUST 27, 1865—Joy to the world—My little world at least. I am no more a war widow—My Precious is home safe from the war. I am so thankful that he is once more home and that to stay. I am happy all the time now. I do not feel now as if I were alone in the world—as I had so often to feel during his three years' absence, and now that the war is over I hope we can once get to our own home and live as God intends we should. We are certainly a happy little family—God grant that we may be a good family too.

From *The Cormany Diaries: A Northern Family in the Civil War*, James C. Mohr, ed., University of Pittsburgh Press, 1982.

The fight to end slavery inspired in Blacks the hope that they would find a secure and equal place in American life. But though the experience of black military service, emancipation, and the pressure of Northern Blacks and their white allies bent racial discrimination, they did not break it. Racism persisted. Sojourner Truth, born a slave in New York State and emancipated by state law in 1828, became a prominent abolitionist and reformer. She helped raise food and clothing for black volunteer regiments and after the war worked in the Freedmen's Hospital in Washington. In this letter of October 1, 1865, to her friend Amy Post, she tells how "the old slaveholding spirit" still lived on:

A FEW WEEKS ago I was in company with my friend Josephine S. Griffing, when the conductor of a streetcar refused to stop his car for me, although [I was] closely following Josephine and holding on to the iron rail. They dragged me a number of yards before she succeeded in stopping them. She reported the conductor to the president of the City Railway, who dismissed him at once, and told me to take the number of the car whenever I was mistreated by a conductor or driver. On the 13th I had occasion to go for blackberry wine, and other necessities for the patients in the Freedmen's Hospital where I have been doing and advising for a number of months. I thought now I would get a ride without trouble as I was in company with another friend, Laura S. Haviland of Michigan. As I ascended the platform of the car, the conductor pushed me, saying "Go back—get off here." I told him I was not going off, then "I'll put you off" said he furiously, clenching my right arm with both hands, using such violence that he seemed about to succeed, when Mrs. Haviland told him he was not going to put me off. "Does she belong to you?" said he in a hurried angry tone. She replied, "She does not belong to me, but she belongs to humanity." The number of the car was noted, and conductor dismissed at once upon the report to the president, who advised his arrest for assault and battery as my shoulder was sprained by his effort to put me off. Accordingly I had him arrested and the case tried before Justice Thompson. My shoulder was very lame and swollen, but is better. It is hard for the old slaveholding spirit to die. But die it must. . . .

From *We Are Your Sisters*, Sterling, Norton, 1984.

Long before the war Lincoln had believed color prejudice was too deeply rooted ever to allow whites and Blacks to live together peacefully as equals. An old admirer of Henry Clay, he had supported the Kentuckian's plan for solving the race problem by shipping free Blacks out of the country. The colonization movement got nowhere: Most Blacks and

189

abolitionists opposed it. As Robert Purvis, the black aboli-
tionist from Philadelphia put it, "The children of the black
man have enriched the soil by their tears, and sweat, and
blood. We were born here, and here we choose to remain."

Projects for emigration collapsed. The North turned to a
new question. Since the Blacks were here to stay, what
would be the place of four million freed slaves in the recon-
structed Union? What kind of new life would the freed
slaves make for themselves? Blacks said it must rest on a
solid base of economic independence. If we have no land of
our own, they said, the white planters will keep us in a state
of semislavery.

But the proposal to break up the Southern plantations
and parcel them out to the landless farmers, black and
white, never became a reality. The government believed it
was too radical, and the hope for a basic change on the land
went glimmering. Though they were defeated in the war,
the Rebels would remain the ruling power in the South.
They lost their slaves, but not their large estates. Would the
freed people have to work for the old master class on their
terms?

Nevertheless the Congress did pass constitutional amend-
ments that changed the status of Blacks. The Thirteenth
Amendment abolished slavery throughout the United
States. The Fourteenth Amendment asserted the equal citi-
zenship of Blacks: They were entitled to the "privileges and
immunities of citizens," to the "equal protection of the
laws," and to protection against being deprived of "life,
liberty and property without due process of law." This
amendment did not include the right of black suffrage.
That was guaranteed in the Fifteenth Amendment, assur-
ing suffrage for all male citizens, regardless of race or color.

(It was the Fourteenth and Fifteenth Amendments that a hundred years later would form the constitutional basis of the civil rights struggle.)

But these were documents, words, promises. And the white South showed immediately that it meant to maintain or restore white supremacy by any means possible, including violence. Two years after repeated terrorist acts against Blacks threatened to wreck the hope of peaceful remaking

Armed members of the Ku Klux Klan. A secret terrorist army, it was formed at the war's end to restore white supremacy in the South by the lash, the torch, and the gun.

Freedmen line up at the polls in the defeated Confederate states, exercising their newly won right to vote.

of the South, Congress adopted a series of Reconstruction Acts that put the Union's military power behind a program to rebuild the South on the basis of freedom, justice, and equality. That effort, which made great advances toward democratic government in all the former Confederate states, lasted only seven years at most. Reconstruction ended in 1877, by a deal made between the Republican and Democratic parties.

There is no room here to go into detail about Reconstruction, its achievements, and its overthrow. It is clear, however, that too many problems were left unsolved in the plans

192

for rebuilding the South. And there were just not enough people, North as well as South, who cared deeply enough about justice for black Americans.

But that is not to say the Civil War was meaningless. The Union was restored, the slaves were freed, and the black people made a great beginning in Reconstruction. They took giant steps away from slavery. They learned to make laws, to plan, to govern, to use power. They became teachers and judges and businessmen and senators. They found out how to organize, and they fought for a better life for all who suffer from injustice and inequality.

FURTHER READING

What has been written about the Civil War runs to hundreds of volumes and many millions of words. Far more men fought in that war than in the American Revolution, and a greater number were literate and moved to leave a record of their experience. On the home front too, the letters and diaries and memoirs exceed in quantity those coming out of any other American war. Even now, more than 125 years after Fort Sumter, documents of the war long forgotten in attics or archives come to light. And the biographies, from the great figures to the more obscure, continue to appear year after year.

For those who wish to read more on the war—its causes, the action, and the aftermath—look into the subject catalog at your library. Under the main heading of "United States—History—Civil War," you'll find nearly twenty large pages of closely printed type in three columns, subdividing the general subject into dozens of subtopics that may catch your interest. It will tell you where to find anything from a politician's speech to a regimental history, from a wartime songbook to the account of a particular battle, from information about black troops to the story of the Copperhead conspiracy. Here I will mention some titles that I think the general reader might find helpful.

The documents I selected to use in this book may be

followed up in the sources given at the end of each section. For those who wish to burrow into more documents, there is *The Blue and the Gray: The Story of the Civil War as Told by Participants,* edited by Henry Steele Commager (Fairfax, 1982). (This is a reprint of the original 1950 edition. While it contains over 450 documents, a great many more have been published in the decades since.) Another useful book is *Life in the North During the Civil War*, edited by George W. Smith (University of New Mexico, 1966). Still another is *The Union Reader*, edited by Richard B. Harwell (Longmans, 1958).

Two superbly detailed books covering every aspect of soldier life are *Life of Johnny Reb* (1943) and *Life of Billy Yank* (1952) by Bell Irwin Wiley, published by Bobbs-Merrill.

A recent book on the war, perhaps the best one-volume treatment thus far, is *Battle Cry of Freedom: The Civil War Era*, by James M. McPherson (Oxford, 1988). Over 900 pages in length, but always absorbing, it is a masterly study of the war in its many aspects. An older and still very popular work is *Bruce Catton's Civil War* (Fairfax, 1984). It is the unabridged one-volume edition of Catton's earlier three volumes, *Mr. Lincoln's Army, Glory Road*, and *A Stillness at Appomattox.* Shelby Foote's *The Civil War* is a three-volume narrative that is rated very highly.

There are many solid biographies of the major war leaders, Lincoln and Jefferson Davis, members of their cabinets, and the state and congressional politicians who influenced policy.

Lincoln is so fascinating a figure that few writers can resist trying to capture him. Carl Sandburg's *Abraham Lincoln: The War Years*, while uncritical, is worth reading for the feeling about the man it conveys so poignantly. More recent biographies include Stephen B. Oates's *With Malice Toward None* and Russell Freedman's *Lincoln: A Photobiography.* For Jefferson Davis see Clement Eaton's biography (1977), or Hudson Strode's three-volume *Jefferson Davis* (1955–64).

General Robert E. Lee's story is told in a definitive multivolume biography by Douglas S. Freeman. There is also Clifford Dowdey's *Lee* (1965). General Ulysses S. Grant wrote his own now classic *Personal Memoirs*, available today in several editions. For a recent and thorough biography see William McFeely's *Grant* (1981). Lives of Jackson, Sheridan, Sherman, Howard, Longstreet, Early, Hood, Thomas, Stuart, Halleck, McClellan, and many other generals continue to appear. In a huge four-volume work called *Battles and Leaders of the Civil War* (reissued in 1956), Union and Confederate officers tell their stories.

Lives of the abolitionists, black and white, are numerous, as are studies of the Southern secessionists. The role of black leaders such as Frederick Douglass is of course of great importance, and biographies and collections of their speeches and writings are available. For accounts of their military role see *The Sable Arm*, by Dudley T. Cornish (1966); *Marching Toward Freedom: The Negro in the Civil War*, by James McPherson (Knopf, 1965); *The Negro in the Civil War*, by Benjamin Quarles (Little, Brown, 1953), and *Army Life in a Black Regiment*, by Thomas W. Higginson (reissued in several editions). There are numerous books on slavery before and during the Civil War.

If you are interested in what the soldiers of your own town or state did in the war, look up the regimental histories of your community.

Pictorial works are a rich source of contemporary evidence. You will see how soldiers and civilians of that day looked in almost every aspect of their lives, at home and on the battlefield. Photography had been invented only some twenty years before the war began, and cameramen roamed everywhere for pictures. Artists too, including the great Winslow Homer, traveled with the armies and made sketches on the spot. See *The Civil War: The Artists' Record*, by H. W. Williams (1962); Julian Grossman's *Echo of a Distant Drum: Winslow Homer and The Civil War* (1974); and Frederic Ray's *Alfred P. Waud, Civil War Artist* (1974).

Broad pictorial coverage can be found in such books as *The American Heritage Picture History of the Civil War* (1960); Paul Angle's *A Pictorial History of the Civil War Years* (1967); Lamont Buchanan's *A Pictorial History of the Confederacy* (1951); Hirst Milholland and Milton Kaplan's *Divided We Fought* (1956); Francis T. Miller's *The Photographic History of the Civil War* (1911); and the series of illustrated books entitled *The Civil War* (Time-Life, 1983).

For some of the greatest photography of the Civil War era look up the work of two masters, Mathew B. Brady and Timothy O'Sullivan. Books are *Mr. Lincoln's Camera Man, Mathew Brady*, edited by Roy Meredith (1946), and Meredith's *Mr. Lincoln's Contemporaries* (1951), which contains many superb Brady portraits of the leading political and military figures of the Civil War years. James D. Horan combined biography with a large selection of photographs in *Timothy O'Sullivan, America's Forgotten Photographer* (1966).

198

INDEX

(Page references to illustrations and their captions are in *italics*.)

abolitionists, *8*, *13*, 73, 79, 188, 190
"Age of Shoddy," 113–16
Alcott, Louisa May, 136–39
Alexandria, 53
American Revolution, 4
Amish, 126, 127
Andersonville prison, 129–34, *133*
Andrews, Eliza, 173–75
Atlanta, 169, 172

Banks, Nathaniel P., 79
Bartlett, Napier, 101–3
"Battle Hymn of the Republic," 58–59
battles *49*, *63*, *64*: Antietam, 67–69; Ball's Bluff, 48–50; Bull Run, 42–46 *45* ; Chickamauga, 163; Cold Harbor, 166; Fredericksburg, 69–72, *71*; Gaines' Mill, 62–65; Gettysburg, 94–102; Lookout Mountain, 164; Milliken's Bend, 81–82; Missionary Ridge, 164; *Monitor* vs. *Merrimack*, 89–93; New Hope Church, 168–69; Port Hudson, 79–80, 158, 163;

Second Bull Run, 67; White Oak Swamp, 65–67
Bishop, Thomas, 58
Blackford, Susan Lee, 145–46
Booth, John Wilkes, 183
Breckinridge, John, 25
Brooklyn, 86–88
Brown, John, 20–23, *22*, 25
Buchanan, James, 16
Buell, Augustus, 94–96
Bull Run, 42–46, *45*
Burnside, Ambrose E., 69

Calhoun, John C., 11, 25
California, 8, 9, 10, 11
Chamberlain, Joshua L., 70–72
Chattanooga, 164–65
Child, Lydia Maria, 53–55
Christian Recorder, 86
Church of the Brethren, 126
Civil War: balance of forces in, 4, 46–47; begins, 33; black troops in, 78–82, *81*, *163* causes of, 3; desertions in, 120–25, *121*; discipline in, 119–25; duration of, 46; effect of Emancipation on, 73–74; losses from

199

Griffing, Josephine S., 188
Grovenor, Gurdon, 153–57

Haley, John, 120–22
Halleck, Henry W., 79
Hancock, Cornelia, 56–57
Harper, Frances E. W., 21
Harpers Ferry raid, 22, 30
Harper's Monthly, 112–13
Haviland, Laura S., 189
Hawthorne, Nathaniel, 27–30
Hood, John B., 169
Hopedale Community, 128–29
Howe, Julia Ward, 58–59
Hudson, Charles, 9
Hunter, David, 79

Indiana, 36–39
Iowa, 107, 127

Jackson, Thomas "Stonewall," 47–48
Jacobs, Harriet, 52–53
Jim Crow streetcars, 188–89
Johnston, Joseph E., 36, 168
Jones, John B., 109–12

Kansas, 16, 18, 128, 153–57, 154
Kansas-Nebraska Act, 16, 18
Keeler, William F., 89–93
Kline, John, 126–27
Know-Nothings, 16

Lane, Jim, 79
Lee, Robert E., 62, 64, 67, 69, 94, 95, 96, 101, 183, 166, 168, 179, 180, 183
liberation songs, 76–78
Liberator, The, 52

Lincoln, Abraham, 28, 74, 185; assassination of, 183–87; blockades Confederacy, 89; calls for Union volunteers, 33; contrasted with Davis, 26; debates Douglas, 19; described by Hawthorne, 27–30; Gettysburg Address, 103–4; "House Divided" speech, 17; issues Emancipation Proclamation, 73; loses Senate race, 20; makes Grant supreme commander, 166; replaces McClellan, 69; second inaugural address of, 179; supports colonization of blacks, 189
Lincoln, Mary Todd, 183–84
Lincoln, Robert, 186
Livermore, Mary, 106–8
Livermore, Thomas, 65–67
Lockwood, L. C., 54
Longfellow, Henry W., 20
Lynchburg, 145
Lyons, Maritchka, 87–88

Maine, 42
Maryland, 60, 67
Massachusetts, 39, 128
McClellan, George B., 51, 62, 64, 67, 69
McKim, Randolph, 96–97
Meade, George Gordon, 94, 101
medical care, 52–53, 56–57, 135–46
Mennonites, 126, 127, 128
Mexican War, 7, 9, 38
Mills, Luther R., 166–67

201

202